The Cafés of Paris

The Cafés of Paris

... a Guide

BY CHRISTINE GRAF

CONSTABLE · LONDON

Copyright © Interlink Publishing Group, Inc., 1996
Text copyright © Christine Graf, 1996
Originally published in the USA by Interlink Books,
an imprint of Interlink Publishing Group Inc.
This edition first published in Great Britain 1998
by Constable and Company Ltd
3 The Lanchesters, 162 Fulham Palace Road
London W6 9ER
ISBN 0 09 477470 6
The right of Christine Graf to be identified as the author
of this work has been asserted by her in accordance with
the Copyright, Designs and Patents Act, 1988

Printed in Great Britain by
St Edmundsbury Press Ltd
Bury St Edmunds, Suffolk

A CIP catalogue record for this book
is available from the British Library

This book is dedicated to my mother
Mary Evans Armstrong (1911–1993):
I miss her.

Contents

Contents

List of Maps

Acknowledgements

To my husband, Dennis Graf whose enthusiasm for France and the French has made Paris a regular part of our lives, to Diane Birkbichler, Sheila Coxe, Judith Dean, Ray Hathaway, Jennifer Nelson, Peter O'Brien, Karen and Steve Soderman, and David Shumway. Special thanks are due to my editors, Phyllis Bennis, Claire Evans and Katherine McCracken.

Among the people whose contributions make up "Parisians Discuss their Favorite Cafés," Stephen Bensimon, Masha Ciardi-Navoret, and Géva Mangin furnished particularly interesting opinions. In addition, Stephen supplied invaluable information about clochards which I have used as background to "The Ratman of Paris." Renée Couffin and Bernadette Saunier have contributed greatly to my knowledge of France. Other Parisians and residents of Paris whose contributions were helpful include Michèle Dedours, Christine Estruga, Imke Glockauer and Alexandra Dickmann, Jérôme Houix, Terry James, Marie Louise Le Reste, Charles and Katherine McCracken, Christophe Sigel and

Acknowledgments

Stéphanie Warin and many other Parisians whose full names I do not know. Anita and Albert Cesbron, Marie Louise Le Reste and Bob Sigel opened their homes, giving encouragement and a base for work in Paris.

Among the teachers at Open University in Minneapolis, Jim Poynter, Jack Caravela, Pat Bell, and Jack Kremer; and finally, in memory of Miss Ethel Evans, of the Rhos, Pembrokeshire, Wales, and Mr. George Barnet, of Milestone, Saskatchewan, Canada and Oxford, England.

Introduction

"Paris is the café of Europe," said the Abbé Galiani, and it is true. What makes the café such an institution in this city? For the average Parisian, the local café can be the equivalent of a private club. It's a place to meet friends and relax at the end of the day, or to have that first cup of espresso to get going in the morning.

If you're visiting Paris, a café can be your way to discover the city. Even when you're only staying for a few days, take the opportunity to find a good neighborhood café near your hotel. After you've gone there a couple of times, you'll begin to feel at home. In a well-run café, you will be greeted as you enter and acknowledged again when you leave. Your cup of coffee or drink will entitle you to hours in which you can rest your feet, write your postcards, and collect your thoughts.

For the tourist on a budget, getting to know the cafés is a must. Many offer delicious coffee in an elegant or historic setting for just a few francs. At lunchtime, a sandwich or a well-prepared entrée will keep you going until evening—at a price that most restaurants can't touch. Most of us may not be able to afford a meal at La Tour d'Argent, Maxim's, Lasserre, or the other *temples de gastronomie*—but there will be a nearby café from which we can enjoy the same view while savoring a good simple meal prepared with French competence and imagination at a fraction of the price.

Much of my information about cafés has come from the French themselves. Renée, a Frenchwoman from Quimper in Brittany, told me about the feelings she had when she first went to live in Paris. She said, "I never thought I'd ever live and work there." The capital city was a terrifying prospect. At first she felt completely alone, an outsider, isolated in her tiny studio apartment and knowing no one. A turning point in her feelings about the city came one morning on her way to work, when she stopped at a café. She had gone there once or twice before to order the typical café-and-croissant breakfast. This time the barman almost smiled; he brought the coffee and croissant with a flourish and a "*voilà, mademoiselle!*" as he set them down. She had not uttered a word. From that time on she felt that in a sense she belonged in Paris. She had found her café.

Bernadette, a friend from the Champagne region in the north of France, now lives near Aix-en-Provence, in the south. She likes to compare the two regions: "There is more of a welcome in the cafés of Paris than in the ones here in Provence," she says. Despite appearances and the popular image of an exotic, sunny paradise in the South, the easygoing Southerner can be difficult to get to know. It will usually take longer to be accepted in the South than in the North. Yet in and around Paris, where people are traditionally considered reserved, the cafés can be oases of welcome. They can make the difference to an outsider trying to find his or her way in the city. The camaraderie, the warmth, the easy banter of conversations in many of the better cafés create an ambiance that is worth seeking out.

Some of it is in the etiquette of the café. When you enter a French café, unless the barman is very busy, you will hear the courteous greeting: "*Bonjour m'sieu, m'dame.*" You sit down and are waited on—possibly not at once, but no one is trying to rush you unless you indicate you're in a hurry. You can take your time over coffee and conversation, and when you get up to leave, there is the polite: *"Au 'voir m'sieur, m'dame."* This routine courtesy creates the kind of atmosphere worth looking for—it may totally transform your perception of the city.

So the café persists, not merely to dispense drinks, but as a place where people can meet each other regularly. It gives Parisians a chance to catch up on the day's events, to find out what's going on in politics, in sports, and in their acquaintances' lives. The talk—the *bavardage*—or gossip, the savoring of the moment as only the French know how to do it, this is what creates the ambiance of a café.

Why Are There Several Different Prices?

A practical point: why do many if not most cafés offer drinks at three different prices? How is the bewildered tourist—who may not know much French—to deal with this?

On the list of the *Tarif des Consommations*, usually visible from the street, the lowest price indicated is for the customer standing at the bar. He or she is occupying little space, will doubtless leave in a few minutes, and therefore deserves the minimum price. For patrons seated at the tables inside, the price can be significantly higher. The third or highest price is for the people with seats at tables outside or on the *terrasse* of the café. They can see what's going on and admire the passersby.

So don't be upset if you find you're being charged more than the minimum amount on the *Tarif des Consommations*. Chances are you preferred to sit down and take in the ambiance of the café. Sometimes the difference between the various prices of coffee can be startling. A pleasant café on the rue Saint-Honoré, across from Georg Jensen, charges 6 francs to people standing or seated in the comfortable barstools, and 13 francs to those drinking their coffee at a table a few feet away.

Prices are even higher at famous cafés in the fashionable

parts of town, so give the *Tarif* a good, hard look before you decide where to stop.

Tea: in a typical café, you pay double the price of coffee for a teabag and water that used to be hot. So while in Paris you may decide to forego tea for a time, or try a *salon de thé*, where the tea is good—but prices are still high.

Tipping: although the service charge is figured into restaurant and café bills, you may want to leave a franc or two, depending on your bill. An English lady I know has no intention of ever forgiving the French nation for something that happened to her right after a reform of the coinage—which she had somehow not managed to understand or appreciate. She was at the railway station and had just tipped her porter in *centimes* (the gold-colored coins, worth a few pennies) rather than in francs. The unfortunate porter had just carried her heavy luggage. He glanced at the almost worthless centimes she had put in his hand and hurled them on the ground with the ringing cry: "Not enough!" She said she had never been so humiliated in her life. To avoid this sort of embarrassment, it is worth taking the time to figure out the currency and to be prepared to give a fair amount to the people who give you good service. After all, it's their livelihood.

Getting Organized

"Order is Heaven's first law,"—Alexander Pope

Getting ready for a trip to Paris involves more than buying your traveller's checks and making sure your passport is up-to-date. You'll want to know the best ways of getting from café to café, or from one famous monument to another—and how to find your hotel again.

Buy a good map: the ones available in book form are the easiest to use, so you won't be struggling to keep a large, unwieldy folding map from getting drenched in a sudden downpour or flying off in a gust of wind.

What is the best way to get around in Paris? The easiest and cheapest method is by bus and métro, just as the Parisians do. In my opinion, it is better to avoid the highly publicized "tourist's passes" which are for sale for a one-, three-, or five-day period. Take along a few small identification photos, and use them when you buy a *Carte Orange.*

The *Carte Orange*, available for sale in métro stations, is good for a week or a month and is an incredible bargain. Recently such a pass, allowing for a week's unlimited travel on the métro or buses of Paris, cost only 75 francs. The pass for a month is even more economical. You show the *Carte* to bus drivers as you enter the bus—do not stamp or *composte* it, as that renders it useless in the métro. Once you're down in the métro, you insert your little ticket or *billet* into the slot that allows you passage through the turnstile, and remember to take the ticket back when it pops up again.

I have learned through experience that the weekly pass is a good buy even if I've only four days to spend in Paris. Conversely, the "free" one-day tourist passes that are sometimes offered as a bonus to travellers buying the France Railpass—an excellent value in itself—are often not worth bothering with. The time you spend lining up at the Gare du Nord for a "free" pass could have been better spent seeing the city with a week's worth of *Carte Orange.*

If you've only a day or two for Paris, and can't justify the *Carte Orange* to yourself, buy a *carnet* of 10 métro tickets. (Just say: *"Un carnet de dix, s'il vous plaît,"* to the ticket seller at the métro station). These tickets can also be used on the bus.

The great feature of the *Carte Orange* is not merely the saving of money. In most cases you save time. No more lining up at métro stations. No more having to avoid entrances where tickets are not for sale. Some métro entrances are marked as only for the use of *passagers munis de billets,* or people who already have tickets: armed with a *Carte Orange*, you can use them too.

What if you're in a rush with no time to buy a ticket? Should you hop over the turnstiles as you see some people doing? Not at all. Don't risk it. Take your time and be legal. The RATP authorities conduct random searches through métro cars. They are unmerciful and have police-like powers: the fine imposed for trying to avoid buying a 5-franc pass would exceed the cost of a month's *Carte Orange*. The low prices of public transportation in Paris are that way because they are subsidized by the taxpayers. The French are already paying for part of your ride: do the right thing and pay the rest.

While you're in Paris, take the time to check out the buses. They are a little harder to figure out than the métro—a colleague's twelve-year-old daughter was riding the métro with perfect ease after two days in Paris—but they are worth the effort, if only because you'll get to see more of the city. And that is why you're there, isn't it? Free bus maps are available at the information booths at the major métro stations. I got into the habit of always taking bus number 20 from the Place de la République to the Grands Magasins, getting off in front of Au Printemps and then walking to the Place de Madeleine—going from a less chic *quartier* to one of the most fashionable in the city. It is fascinating to see the changes along the way. Some of the dirt and grime in the now disreputable Saint-Denis area conceals stunning façades in the turn-of-the-century, Belle Epoque style.

Money

"There are few certainties when you travel. One of them is that the moment you arrive in a foreign country, the American dollar will fall like a stone."—Erma Bombeck

For travellers who have found Erma's words only too true, there

are still ways of dealing with a vacation in which the dollar or
the pound seems headed in only one direction and that is down.
One of the most important principles to follow is to be very
careful about where you go to change money.

Many people visiting Europe make Thomas Cook or American Express their headquarters. This is a long tradition, dating
from the days when F. Scott Fitzgerald and e.e. cummings used
to go there hoping for encouraging news or a cheque from home.
The American Express office may be a good option—if you
happen to be near the Opéra. But it is too well known, and
going there entails joining the invariably long line of people
waiting to change their money. Arthur Frommer used to recommend a moneychanger on the rue Scribe, near American
Express. I think one would have to go a long way to improve
on the rates given by the moneychangers on the rue Vivienne,
near the Bourse. The rue Vivienne is a short street in front of
the Bourse, and within two blocks are several moneychangers.
The rates of the day are posted in their windows: none charges
a fee or commission for changing money, and all give a much
better than average rate—usually even better than American
Express, and without the long lines.

On the Left Bank, I recently found moneychangers near
the métro Saint-Placide on the rue de Rennes, not far from
the Alliance Française on boulevard Raspail. Here they gave
the same fair rates as those on the rue Vivienne.

Warning: there are conspicuous *change* offices throughout
the city, in all of the main tourist areas: the Champs-Elysées,
the Left Bank, and others. Frequently a large sign advertises
"No commission." What they don't mention is that the rates
given are usually so far below the rate of exchange given by a
reputable moneychanger or bank that the unwary tourist winds
up paying a hefty price for the "convenience" of changing his
or her money then and there. The most conspicuous number
posted will be the high price they are charging the French who
want to buy dollars or pounds, not what they'll give you when

you sell yours. One summer, for example, when reputable dealers were giving almost 6 francs to the dollar, these establishments were offering 5.30 or even less. Avoid them! Make a point of changing your money during regular business hours, so that you can get the best rates offered by the top moneychangers or banks. Among the French banks, the Banque de France, with branches throughout the country, will generally offer reasonable rates, especially for traveller's cheques.

The Language

"Comment allez-vous? . . . my wife speaks good French, I understand only one out of every five words . . ."—John F. Kennedy, greeting the wife of the French Ambassador at a White House dinner.

You may feel just as much at sea with the French language as JFK did—but if you want to get the most out of your trip to Paris, it helps if you make an effort to say a few words in French. Kennedy himself managed to say "How are you?" Little phrases like this make the difference between appearing to be the worst kind of tourist or a traveller of some sophistication. The Berlitz phrasebooks and cassettes can be of great help.

Times have changed since Mark Twain wrote in *Paris Notes*:

The Parisian travels but little, he knows no language but his own, reads no literature but his own, and consequently he is pretty narrow and pretty self-sufficient. However, let us not be too sweeping; there are Frenchmen who know languages not their own; these are the waiters.

Over the years we have noticed in Paris a change in Parisians' attitudes towards speaking English. In the past, many French people would have studied English at school and yet feel reluctant to admit it. When you'd get to know them well enough to discuss the subject, they'd say their school courses focused on grammar and translation, and that it was impossible to learn to speak a foreign language in a class of forty that met two or three times a week. They could imagine themselves making hilarious gaffes. But more recently a new generation of young Parisians has appeared. These younger people are often eager to practice their language skills. Workers in fast-food places, the French equivalent of MacDonald's, have insisted on addressing me in rather good English when I wanted to practice my French. More and more of the young people have gone on *séjours linguistiques* or language-learning stays in Britain and the U.S., and enjoy using their English.

Still, you will get more out of your trip if you brush up on your French or learn a few phrases for the first time. A simple greeting, "*Bonjour*," or, in the evening, "*Bonsoir*," always used with "*monsieur*" or "*madame*," will smooth your way. If you need complicated explanations, efforts will be made to find an English-speaking person for you to talk to.

An American living in Hong Kong once told us how Leonard Bernstein used to deal with the language barrier when he had to order dinner in a Paris restaurant:

He would start out with rapid fire New York slang. The waiter, totally at sea, would summon another waiter, who was equally dumbfounded by this incomprehensible jabber. They would make heroic efforts to understand, calling in someone from the kitchen who was rumored to know some English. Bernstein's response: to babble faster and faster. The maître d' would appear. Complete bewilderment on every face—was Monsieur speaking English? Finally Bernstein would relent: in schoolboy French, heavily accented and very slow, he would start to order again. By then everybody was so relieved that his efforts were met with warm smiles and great praise for his "mastery" of the language.

But this strategy is not necessary in the friendlier Paris of today. Try to learn and use a few key phrases and to see more of the real Paris of the Parisians in some of their small neighborhood cafés—this will keep you from experiencing the kind of isolation described by Canadian humorist Stephen Leacock:

> The traveller of today "sees France" by tearing through it in a closed car over a straight cement highway at the rate of sixty miles an hour; by stopping in "international" hotels run in imitation of American methods . . . and, as a diversion, playing bridge with other English-speaking tourists and looking at American moving pictures and English newspapers.

The French: Politesse

"Courtesy is fine and heaven knows we need more and more of it in a rude and frenetic world, but mechanized courtesy is as pallid as Pablum . . . in fact, it isn't even courtesy. One can put up with 'Service with a Smile' if the smile is genuine and not mere compulsory tooth baring."—Cornelia Otis Skinner

In Paris, you will not see as much of the "compulsory toothbaring" that the British and the Americans have come to accept as a necessary part of their dealings when they go out in public. It is not considered important to put on a "happy face" when dealing with people, although most French people behind the counter are polite. The French do not lack friendliness towards outsiders—in fact, they often display a real interest and curiosity. When people smile, it's usually for a reason. Smiles that you see tend to be genuine. So do not feel offended if the person waiting on you doesn't give you a big smile; he or she is not necessarily angry or in a bad mood! The smile is not obligatory in France and is not part of the training people undergo when learning the retail trades.

"Tourists can do whatever they want," said Géva, one of my former professors, and to some extent this is true. I can't quite remember what prompted the remark: someone may have committed a social gaffe, like cutting the "nose" off a Brie cheese. Who knows? But Géva affirmed that people are ready to give an outsider the benefit of the doubt. You may wonder what's appropriate: is it, for example, all right to strike up a conversation with people you encounter in a café or restaurant? Remember, you're a visitor to the country and your time is limited. You may not be able to get to know the barman or proprietor of your favorite café well enough for him to introduce you to regular customers. But keep this in mind: the fussy French often appreciate the efforts one makes at conversation. Sometimes too inhibited to start talking to you themselves, they may welcome the opportunity to meet a visitor to their country. They will probably have questions they've been dying to ask the "typical" American or Briton, just as you have some you've been saving up for a native. Of course, it's important to use a measure of tact and common sense: this is not the time to launch into a condemnation of France and the French! But a little honest appreciation can go a long way in breaking down barriers and deepening your understanding and appreciation of the country. Your openness, your readiness to meet new people and learn new things, can count for a lot. As Theodore Dreiser put it, "Paris and the Riviera are great realities—there are houses and crowds and people and great institutions and the remembrance and flavor of great deeds; but the one thing that you get out of all this . . . is born of the attitude or mood which you take with you."

Map of the Arrondissements

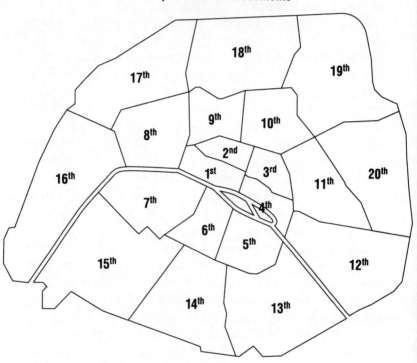

1

The American Cafés: Montparnasse and the 6th Arrondissement

"It is easier to be happy in Paris, probably, than anywhere else in this modern machine world: it is very easy in June: with a little luck, it is easiest of all in Montparnasse."—Harold Stearns

You could be sitting in the café where Ernest Hemingway wrote *The Sun Also Rises*. You could have coffee where Henry James met Turgenev. In Paris, it is possible to walk in the footsteps of some of the greatest Americans of this and earlier centuries. If this prospect sounds appealing, *les cafés américains* will suit you. These establishments proliferated on the Left Bank of Paris during the 1920s. Many of them are still there, serving up espresso and fulfilling our need to experience an important part of America's literary history.

Thomas Jefferson knew Paris in 1780. He was sent there to join Benjamin Franklin and John Adams in negotiating trade with Europe. He remained in Europe when Franklin went back to America in July of 1785. When people asked him if he was the replacement for Franklin, Jefferson would answer: "No one can replace him, Sir; I am only his successor."

In his meticulously kept account book, Jefferson noted that he paid 24 francs for dinner near the Palais Royal. At the **Café de Foy**, he played chess in the **Salon des Echecs** on February 6, 1786, having paid 96 francs to enter the Salon.

"Writing in Paris is one of the oldest American customs," said Van Wyck Brooks, and at no time was that more true than in the 1920s. It was to Paris that would-be young writers flocked then—people whose names were to become famous: Ernest Hemingway, F. Scott Fitzgerald, Henry Miller, Ezra Pound, and others. Some had already attained celebrity at home. Sinclair Lewis, already known in America for *Main Street* and *Babbitt*, sat and sulked at the **Café du Dôme** while other writers conspicuously ignored him: they looked down on the writer of mere best-sellers. According to observers at the time, Lewis's face soon took on the tones of his sandy-colored hair, and he stamped out in a rage—much to the glee of his less successful contemporaries.

But Lewis had already been to Paris. On his first trip to the City of Light, he did not impress anyone with his high level of culture: in 1921, with writer and editor Harold Stearns, he set out for a three-day drunk, a "clamorous and memorably boozy entry into Paris," according to Hugh Ford. He and Stearns took the boat train, the channel ferry, and the fast train into the capital, downing every drink they could lay hands on along the way.

Once in Paris, they went to the **Dôme**, where they sat with Malcolm Cowley. Cowley remembered later that Lewis, already quite intoxicated, kept on ordering drinks, pounding his cane on the table and shouting: "Garcong! Garcong! Come here, you bloody garcong!" Afterwards, Lewis recalled that he had enjoyed the short trip to Paris, and wrote that Stearns would have "an ever widening future" as a writer.

Four years later, Sinclair Lewis had completely changed his assessment of his former drinking companion and of the Amercian café scene in general. Lewis wrote that the "standardized rebels" from America had changed the **Dôme**: "Among ... other advantages of the Dôme, it is on a corner charmingly resembling Sixth Avenue at Eighth Street, and all the waiters understand Americanese, so that it is possible for the patrons to be highly expatriate without benefit of Berlitz. It is, in fact, the perfectly standardized place to which standardized rebels flee from the crushing standardization of America." Stearns was said to be an authority on "literature, painting, music, economics, and living without laboring."

The **Dôme** was described by Geoffrey Fraser in the *Paris Tribune* as being more than a place:

It is an atmosphere. And no one has ever succeeded in describing an atmosphere .... You sit, ensconced in a corner, sipping an apéritif—or if editors have been unkind lately, a café crème. Tags of conversation reach you, floating down with the smoke of cigarettes ...

An old man comes in, hatless, stumpy, with greyish hair and beard, fine eyes and a laughing mouth ...

"Who's that?"

"Don't know his name—only thing I do know is he hasn't had a room these last 8 years."

"No room? Where does he sleep?"

"In cafés here and there. They all know him around here."

.... I remember once catching a glimpse of one of the world's richest men; a little, crabbed, wizened old creature, sour discontent etched on his face. And this homeless old man is radiating with happiness and love.

Hemingway was later to model the character of Harvey Stone in *The Sun Also Rises* on Harold Stearns:

3

I walked past the sad tables of the Rotonde to the Sélect. There were a few people inside at the bar, and outside, alone, sat Harvey Stone. He had a pile of saucers in front of him, and he needed a shave.

"Sit down," said Harvey. "I've been looking for you."

"What's the matter?"

"Nothing. Just looking for you."

"Been out to the races?"

"No. Not since Sunday."

"What do you hear from the States?"

"Nothing. Absolutely nothing."

"What's the matter?"

"I don't know. I'm through with them. I'm absolutely through with them."

He leaned forward and looked me in the eye.

"Do you want to know something, Jake?"

"Yes."

"I haven't had anything to eat for five days."

Writing to F. Scott Fitzgerald, who had been wanting to help Stearns, Hemingway condemned the latter as a has-been who had done nothing for two years and whom it was useless to try to reform: "A gent who's drinking himself to death ought not to be constantly having to raise the funds to do it with. I do think Harold had a pretty damned good head. Also think he destroyed it or completely covered it with fuzz by drinking."

"Paris was where the twentieth century was."—Gertrude Stein

Why did people like Stearns, aspiring American writers, feel they had to go to Paris in the 1920s? The most obvious answer is money. Exchange rates were very favorable; a rate of 25 francs to the dollar is sometimes mentioned. Eighty dollars bought a tourist-class ticket across the Atlantic. This meant that struggling writers could often live more cheaply in Paris than at home.

4

To people familiar with Paris today, the prices seem like a wild fantasy: in the late 1920s, a three-course meal could be had for 20 cents.

Some Americans also went to revel in the unaccustomed feeling of freedom that they found in Paris. This was a longstanding reaction to the French capital. Emerson in 1848 and Richard Wright in 1946 both commented on the greater sense of personal liberty they experienced there. Washington Irving and James Fenimore Cooper were two famous writers who spent years living in Paris early in the nineteenth century. After the First World War it was possible to live well there on $1500 a year.

So to Paris they flocked in the 1920s, with 23-year-old Ernest Hemingway at their head, knocking at the door of Gertrude Stein at 27 rue de Fleurus. Paris was to be the place where young Americans developed as writers, and this was never more true than in the 1920s.

The cafés of Montparnasse were the centers and meeting places for American writers. Montparnasse was "a weird little land, crowded with artists, alcoholics, prostitutes, pimps, poseurs, college boys, tourists, society slummers, spendthrifts, beggars, homosexuals, drug addicts, nymphomaniacs, sadists, masochists, thieves, gamblers, confidence men, mystics, fakers, paranoiacs, political refugees, anarchists . . . men and women without a country. A land filled with a gaiety sometimes real and often feigned," recalled Samuel Putnam, a writer who was living in Paris at the time.

The **Dôme**, the **Sélect**, and the **Coupole** were the usual haunts of Americans who had made Paris their home. The **Dôme** had evolved from a tiny bistro on the corner of the boulevard Raspail and the boulevard du Montparnasse. The word "bistro" dates from the Russian occupation of Paris in 1814. Russian Cossacks would shout "Bistro! Bistro!" ("Quickly! Quickly!") in an effort to hurry up the waiters.

Among the cafés in the 1920s, the **Deux Magots**, according to Samuel Putnam, was neutral ground between opposing camps and the Right and Left Banks of Paris. Although the **Deux Magots** is associated with Ernest Hemingway, in *A Moveable Feast,* he tells of avoiding it and other so-called "American" cafés. He preferred to work at home or where he was not well known. Other writers, too, had soon sensed the potential dangers and temptations of life in Paris. "Paris really is a test for an American," wrote Hart Crane. It was too much of a test for some.

In one episode recalled in *A Moveable Feast,* Hemingway avoids the **Deux Magots** and seeks out another place to write:

> I . . . crossed the rue de Rennes so that I would not go to the Deux-Magots for coffee and was walking up the rue Bonaparte on the shortest way home. I went up Bonaparte to Guynemer, then to the rue d'Assas, up the rue Notre-Dame-des-Champs to the Closerie des Lilas. I sat in a corner with the afternoon light coming in over my shoulder and wrote in the notebook. The waiter brought me a café crème.

Later he mentioned that the **Closerie des Lilas** was the nearest good café to his and Hadley's apartment on the rue Notre-Dame-des-Champs. For them it was one of the best cafés in Paris, with tables under the shade of trees on the side with the statue of Marshal Ney. Hemingway found in the **Closerie** an escape from the usual American crowd that had come to dominate the **Dôme** and the **Rotonde**. These people were there, he thought, more to see and be seen than for any other reason.

Coping with winter in small Parisian apartments, invariably without central heating, was a problem for Americans used to a certain standard of comfort. For Ernest Hemingway, a café was a congenial place to go on writing as the weather grew colder: "Alone there was no problem when you got used to [the weather]. I could always go to a café to write and could work all morning over a café crème while the waiters cleaned and swept out the café and it gradually grew warmer."

But the arrival of Bumby, the Hemingways' baby, finally 'drove them out of Paris: "Our Paris was too cold for him," wrote Ernest.

In *A Moveable Feast* the writer leaves us with the impression that while he and some others spent their time in Paris polishing their craft, F. Scott Fitzgerald gave up too many of his potentially creative hours drinking in the cafés and cabarets. Much later, Dorothy Parker contradicted this idea in an interview published in the *Paris Review*:

> Gertrude Stein did us the most harm when she said, "You're all a lost generation." That got around to certain people and we all said, "Whee! We're lost." Perhaps it suddenly brought to us the sense of change. Or irresponsibility. But don't forget that, though the people in the twenties seemed like flops, they weren't. Fitzgerald, the rest of them, reckless as they were, drinkers as they were, they worked damned hard and all the time.

A similar view was held by the Canadian writer Morley Callaghan. In *That Summer in Paris* he described his friendship with both Fitzgerald and Hemingway during some memorable months in 1929. His and his wife Loretto's life in Paris came to center on their time in the "American" cafés:

> On one corner was the Dôme, which not long ago had been merely a zinc bar with a small terrace; now it was like the crowded bleachers at an old ball park, the chairs and tables . . . extending as far as the next café, the Coupole. It had an even longer crowded terrace . . . . We sat at the Coupole. The faces in rows there looked more international, whereas at the Dôme there seemed to be hundreds of recognizable Americans . . .
> When we had had our fill of the faces and the snatches of conversation at the Coupole, we strolled along the boulevard

as far as the Closerie des Lilas. How lovely the lighted tables looked that April night; a little oasis of conviviality! Apollinaire's café.

Soon the café scene became indispensable to the Callaghans:

> Now that we were established we fell into a routine. We would get up around noon, walk slowly over to the Coupole, have a little lunch on the terrace, then go across to the river to the American Express to inquire for mail. Sometimes we loafed around the Right Bank for hours, having a drink at some café by the Opera, or the Madeleine.

At night he and Loretto would go to the Coupole for an *apéritif.* Hemingway had wanted to develop his boxing skills; he managed to talk Callaghan into acting as a sparring partner. Sometimes after a sparring match he and Callaghan would go up to the **Sélect** and meet Loretto there. Hemingway's new wife, Pauline, had made it clear that she had no interest in sitting around at cafés, but Loretto and Morley enjoyed them.

Hemingway by now was shunning cafés most of the time, preferring not to waste his days there. He had seen the phenomenon of the failed American writer in Paris more than once. In *The Sun Also Rises* he describes what could and did often happen:

> You're an expatriate. You've lost touch with the soil. You get precious. Fake European standards have ruined you. You drink yourself to death. You spend all your time talking, not working. You are an expatriate, see? You hang around cafés.

Yet Hemingway appreciated the good Alsatian cooking available at the **Brasserie Lipp**, near Place Saint-Germain-des-Prés. His enjoyment of the sensual pleasures of the table comes out in his description of a simple meal:

... I asked for a big glass mug that held a liter, and for potato salad. The beer was very cold and wonderful to drink. The pommes à l'huile were firm and marinated and the olive oil delicious. I ground black pepper over the potatoes and moistened the bread in the olive oil. After the first heavy draft of beer I drank and ate very slowly ...

The cafés of the Left Bank provide the setting for memorable stories about other American writers. One was Henry Miller. For hours he would expound his personal philosophy, having to do with the relative purity of prostitutes in an impure world. One day one of his less patient listeners couldn't stand it any longer and exploded: "For Christ's sake, Hank, why don't you write a book?" He did, and the rest, as they say, is history. Samuel Putnam remembered Miller as "a good drinking companion, a nice guy to run into at Jimmy's or the Coupole or in those desolate, shivering hours at the Dôme."

Years later, when he was interviewed for the *Paris Review*, Miller was asked what he had found in Paris in the 1930s that he couldn't find in America:

... I found a freedom such as I never knew in America. I found contact with people so much easier.... I met more of my own kind there. Above all I felt that I was tolerated. I didn't ask to be understood or accepted. To be tolerated was enough. In America I never felt that. But then, Europe was a new world to me. I suppose it might have been good almost anywhere—just to be in some other, different, world, an alien. Because all my life, really ... I've liked only what is alien.

In Paris after a failed marriage, American writer Kay Boyle came to know and appreciate the work of Hart Crane, whom at first she had condemned as "as phlegmatic as a Rotarian, as entertaining as the American Legion." When Crane failed to appear for a visit, she heard that he had been in a brawl at the **Sélect**. Edmond Taylor told readers all about it in the *Paris Tribune* of July 10, 1929:

> Mr. Crane and 'some of his friends had been celebrating the Fourth in a well-known Montparnasse café . . . celebrating it by playing a game . . . which is known as "building castles." The purpose of the game is to erect towers and battlements out of the little white saucers which the café furnishes. When the game was over Mr. Crane looked at his castle and decided that it was too big for him to have built by himself. . . . Accordingly, when the garçon came around to make him pay for his fun, Mr. Crane replied that he hadn't had as much fun as all that and refused to pay the full amount of the bill.
>
> The garçon called a policeman and the policeman, after remonstrating with Mr. Crane, offered him the hospitality of one of the city's handsomest hoosegows. Mr. Crane refused the offer. He loaded down the policeman with a charge of what was described as astonishingly proficient French invective, and wound up . . . by leaping at the man's throat.
>
> In due time he was subdued, but even then his friends helped to complicate things by forming a barricade of autos across the rue Vavin and trying to prevent the police from carrying off their prisoner. Everyone in Montparnasse thought it was a wonderful party and asked the police to drop in again soon, but the next morning Mr. Crane did not think it was so funny. Instead of letting him go with a warning or a small fine as is usually done they held him in jail for another day—then another one.

Art critic and writer Jean-Paul Crespelle, in his study of Montparnasse from 1905 to 1930, saw the great years of the American cafés from a French perspective. He noted that Americans kept the bistros and cafés going but could be difficult to deal with:

... Americans weren't easy customers. Quarrelsome and, contrary to most other foreigners, not suffering from any sense of inferiority faced with these "little Frenchmen" wearing berets, they could be tough customers when they had drunk a few whiskeys too many, something which happened frequently .... The behavior of Americans differed also in another way from that of the first foreigners to come to Montparnasse: they mixed in willingly with French society, something which was even more remarkable when you consider that with the exception of Man Ray, whose French wife had taught him our language "on the pillow," they spoke French badly.

Crespelle noted the large number of talented Americans who made Montparnasse their home in the 1920s:

Besides Hemingway, Miller, Man Ray, Calder, Thompson, who made long stays, one could frequently meet Scott Fitzgerald, Dos Passos, Faulkner, Sherwood Anderson .... Gershwin, who was appreciated and encouraged by Ravel, wrote the music for "An American in Paris" in his hotel room without a piano ...

He recognized the importance of the cafés and the Left Bank in the lives of the expatriate Americans:

We must remember that it was at Lipp's that Hemingway wrote *A Farewell to Arms*, that Ezra Pound wrote, in his studio on rue Notre-Dame-des-Champs, several of his Cantos .... To have an idea of the richness of American cultural life, it is enough to read the memoirs of Kay Boyle and Robert MacAlmon .... the events of these ten years in Paris are among the most fruitful in American literature and music.

11

Where are the legendary cafés, the cafés that were home to some of the major writers of this century? Many of them are still where they always were and are still open. For a closer look at where literary history was made, here are some to investigate:

La Coupole, 102 boulevard du Montparnasse, 75014 Paris (43.20.14.20). Open from noon to 2 a.m. Métro: Vavin. Coffee costs only 6 francs at the bar, 9.50 otherwise, with a *café crème* at twice that price. Full meals are very expensive, but you may want a sandwich—still only 15 to 25 francs. **La Coupole** opened in 1927; Joseph Barry described it as "the place where the Right Bank meets the Left Bank, and comes over expressly to do so." He considered it the best place in Paris "to see French life without leaving your seat, from *la vie bohème* to *la vie bourgeoise*." Forget about intimacy in this vast interior where the bar is blond oak and the decor continues from there in blond oak and light greens. White napkins upthrust on many little tables remind you of the coifs of Breton women. A modern sculpture erupts from the center. The *toilettes* are worth a visit: they're clean and well lighted, in rose and white marble with touches of contrasting green.

La Closerie des Lilas, 171 boulevard du Montparnasse, 75006 Paris (43.26.70.50). Open daily from noon to 1 a.m. Métro: Port-Royal. Here Hemingway wrote most of *The Sun Also Rises*. The Closerie is no longer an inexpensive place for lunch, but you might want to try the *brasserie* section. Coffee costs 15 francs, and a dessert may set you back 45 to 50 francs. A Parisienne we met at La Palette (see "Parisians Discuss Their Favorite Cafés," p. 131) raved about the ambiance of the Closerie.

Le Café du Dôme, 108 boulevard du Montparnasse, 75014 Paris (43.35.25.81). Open between 10 a.m. and 2 a.m. Closed Mondays. Métro: Vavin. Coffee is 15 francs (8 at the bar), and a sandwich about 22. From the elaborate zinc bar you can observe the *banquettes* of light green against dark wood. Dark orange walls resemble an enameled version of the famous Hermès shopping bag. Robert, the friendly, talkative barman, reminisced with us about his twenty-three years at the bar, and mentioned that a host of VIPs are habitués of the Dôme. In summer, the air conditioning can be very welcome.

Les Deux Magots, 170 boulevard Saint-Germain-des-Prés, 75006 Paris (45.48.55.25). Métro: Saint-Germain-des-Prés. Open from 8 a.m. to 1:30 a.m. daily. Closed in August. At both Les Deux Magots and its next-door neighbor, Le Flore, coffee is high priced—22 and 21 francs respectively. A sandwich or a pastry will run from 35 to 40 francs apiece.

Harry's Bar, 5 rue Daunou, 75002 Paris (42.61.71.14). Métro: Opéra. Frequented by Hemingway, Fitzgerald, and their friends, Harry's is said to be the oldest cocktail bar in Europe.

Le Sélect, 99 boulevard du Montparnasse, 75006 Paris (45.48.38.24). Métro: Vavin. Open Sunday to Thursday, from 8 a.m. to 2 a.m.; Friday and Saturday, open until 3:30 a.m. This is a lively café. Le Sélect is said to be relatively unchanged since the days of Hemingway and Fitzgerald—except in its prices! Still, it's a bargain compared to many others. Depending on the time of day, coffee is 6 to 10 francs at the bar, 12 or 15 if you're seated inside; *café crème* is 22 and 24 francs respectively, beer 25 and up, and sandwiches range from 23 to 50 francs. The colors are green, cream and marble, with the typical little brass-edged tables.

Brasserie Lipp, 151 boulevard Saint-Germain, 75006 Paris (45.48.53.91). Métro: Saint-Germain-des-Prés. Another favorite of American writers. Currently frequented by actors, authors and singers. Now, unfortunately, the Lipp is expensive—it would be easy to spend 300 francs per person here in this air-conditioned interior, open until 1 a.m. Coffee can be had for 18 francs.

Hemingway's Bar, Ritz Hotel, 38 rue Cambon, 75001 Paris (42.60.38.30). Métro: Madeleine. "Big splurge" territory, the Ritz was known to Hemingway, who claimed to have "liberated" it in 1944. It was featured in the writings of Hemingway, Fitzgerald, and Ian Fleming, among others: Scott Fitzgerald mentions the "strange and portentous" stillness in the Ritz Bar of 1929 in "Babylon Revisited." Avoid it unless you're feeling flush. The Ritz may be worth a look, although for better value for your money, try the *brasseries* **Flo** and **Bofinger**.

The Rotonde, 105 boulevard Montparnasse, 75006 Paris (43.26.68.84). Opulent-looking today with its deep red interior, the Rotonde was once mentioned in a negative review from Ernest Hemingway. In the March 25 Toronto *Star Weekly* of 1922 he criticized his compatriots: "The gang that congregates at the corner of the Boulevard Montparnasse and the Boulevard Raspail have no time to work at anything else: they put in a full day at the Rotonde."

Au Rendez-vous du Bâtiment, 15 rue d'Assas, 75006 Paris. Métro: Saint-Placide. Convenient to the Institut Catholique, where the July summer school draws francophiles from all over. Pleasant ambiance.

Au Vieux Colombier, 65 rue de Rennes, 75006 Paris (45.48.53.81). Métro: Rennes or Saint-Placide. Au Vieux Colombier is a charming café, with green wood curving in sinuous Art Nouveau shapes to create an impressive façade. Coffee is 5.60 and 12 francs, juice, soda, and mineral water 14 and 20, tea 18, sandwiches 18 to 30 francs, and a *croque monsieur* 26 francs.

Le Calumet, 30 rue Notre-Dame-des-Champs, on the corner of the boulevard Raspail, 75006 Paris. Métro: Notre-Dame-des-Champs. Le Calumet appeals to the "Catho's" main competition in the summer, the nearby Alliance Française. Coffee costs 5 francs at the bar, 10 seated—corresponding prices for fruit juice and soda are 14 and 19 francs. A *pression* (draft beer) is 13.50 at the bar, 19 at a table. They use a high quality bread, *pain poilâne*, in the sandwiches for 14 to 15 francs. The interior of this little café-bar tries to resemble burl walnut. A modern style zinc bar tops slabs of real marble. The coin telephone is handy if you don't have a card, and the barmen are friendly.

Le Boul' Mich, 116 boulevard Saint-Germain, 75006 Paris (46.33.76.66). Métro: Saint-Michel. Le Boul' Mich is on the corner of the rue Danton, rue de l'Eperon and the boulevard Saint-Germain. It has more than average appeal, with yellow Schweppes umbrellas sprouting like flowers over the tables and cane chairs. Coffee is 5.50 and 11 francs, juice and soda 18 and 21, beer 12 and 18, and mineral water 10 and 21.

Le Danton, at 103 boulevard Saint-Germain, 75006 Paris (43.54.65.38). Métro: Odéon. Le Danton is near the statue of its namesake. Traditionally appealing to American students, Le Danton is worth a second look: coffee 5.70 and 11 francs.

Le Tournon, 18 rue de Tournon, 75006 Paris. A simple basic café, with a pinball machine by the door. Still, Le Tournon is mentioned more often than any other in the memoirs of African-American writer Chester Himes. He describes it as the hangout for African-Americans: "Ollie [Oliver Harrington, a cartoonist] became my best friend at the Café Tournon . . . he kept large audiences entertained and drew people to the Tournon to hear him. We could sit all night ad-libbing and never miss a cue." (*My Life of Absurdity*). Novelist Richard Wright would stop by to play the pinball machine. Coffee 5.50 and 10 francs.

Le Pré aux Clercs, at 30 rue Bonaparte, 75006 Paris (43.54.41.73). Métro: Saint-Germain-des-Prés. Le Pré aux Clercs was Hadley Hemingway's favorite café after she separated from Ernest. Give it a try: it is a pleasant little neighborhood café with reasonable prices. Coffee is 6 and 13 francs, tea and most other drinks 13.50 and 21.

Le Saint-André, at 2 rue Danton, on the Place Saint-André-des-Arts, 75006 Paris (43.26.56.59). Just opposite the métro Saint-Michel, Le Saint-André is an attractive café, with its little square tables and classy-looking interior in muted tones of brown. Coffee is 5.50 and 11.50 francs, beer 9.50 and 19, juice and soda 15 and 21, and sandwiches 20 and 29.

Le Trait d'Union, 122 rue de Rennes, 75006 Paris (45.48.70.66). Métro: Saint-Placide. The Trait d'Union is close enough to the Alliance Française and the Institut Catholique to be interesting to the students and professors of both, as well as to shoppers on the rue de Rennes. Here coffee is 5.50 and 10.50 francs, beer 11 and 18, juice and soda 15 and 20, and a sandwich made with *pain poilâne* 14 to 16 francs. The Trait has a modern zinc bar with comfortable barstools. Cane chairs surround the typical small round tables. Service was brisk and efficient, yet pleasant: the barmaid brought a small pot of milk for our coffee without our asking for it. A clean, pleasant, no-nonsense sort of café, even with the pinball machines near the door.

For lunch in this lively area, you may want to consider:

Café le Volcan, 10 rue Thouin, 75005 Paris (46.33.38.33). Métro: Monge or Cardinal LeMoine. Here is Greek food, with a 55-franc menu at lunch including wine. Open from noon to 2 p.m. and from 7 to 11 p.m.

Le Petit Vatel, 5 rue Lobineau, 75006 Paris (43.54.28.42). Métro: Saint-Sulpice or Odéon. There is a 59-franc menu.

Restaurant des Beaux-Arts, 11 rue Bonaparte, 75006 Paris (42.26.92.64). Métro: Saint-Germain-des-Prés. Opposite the Ecole des Beaux-Arts, this restaurant offers a 72-franc menu, with salads going for about 30 francs.

2

Cafés and French Writers in History: Palais Royal—the Tuileries—Grands Boulevards

"The most friendly observer cannot ignore the fact that the consuming ambition of the Parisian is to pose.... He prefers it even to dawdling on the boulevards or making epigrams.... And nowhere can he strike an attitude with more effect than in the café."—Henry Shelley

I f Parisians ever did require places where they could "pose," cafés have long fulfilled this need. The first French café was in Marseille in 1654. Ironically, the true founder of the Parisian café was not French, but a Sicilian from Palermo, Francesco Procopio dei Coltelli. Coltelli opened a café on the rue de

Tournon in 1702. Later he started another at a better address, across from the Comédie Française, where it could appeal to both actors and audience. Possibly because of the location, perhaps because he made his name more French, changing it to François Procope Couteau, this second café was a success.

Coffee was not only known, it was already becoming fashionable among the French aristocracy in the seventeenth century. Writing to her daughter, who had married and moved to Provence, Madame de Sévigné recommended coffee as a remedy for various ailments. In the spring of 1679, she reported that her own health was very good, attributing it to the coffee she was drinking. Fifteen years later, on Monday March 29, 1694, she mentioned enjoying a good laugh at her daughter's expense, referring to a letter in which the young woman had described a mishap over the coffee: "We really laughed about the good Breton salt which looked like sugar, and the care you all took to mix it well with your coffee; the reaction must have been strong, because everybody must have added it to his own cup." Obsessed with the state of her daughter's health, and always fearing the worst, De Sévigné at times recommended not only coffee, but chocolate, tea, and milk for their curative powers.

Cafés became numerous in the first half of the eighteenth century. By 1716, there were more than 300. Coffeehouses became the places for literary and political discussions. Many people went to cafés to play chess, particularly at the **Café de la Régence**. Later on in the century and up to 1789, strict laws were imposed on cafés: they had to close at 9 p.m. in the winter and at 10 p.m. in the summer. No prostitutes, soldiers, vagabonds, or beggars were to be admitted, and no drinks were to be served on Sundays or feast days when people were supposed to be going to mass.

In 1713, Montesquieu made light of café life in *Les Lettres Persanes*. He wrote that coffee was very popular in Paris and that a great number of places distributed it. In some of these places, he said, people spread the news, and in others they play chess. He went on to parody the kinds of subjects that gave rise to fierce arguments among literary men. One such topic concerned the merits of Homer, that "old Greek poet whose birthplace and the time of his death have remained unknown for 2,000 years." Montesquieu asked for divine protection against the anger of people who will not even grant peace to a poet after 2,000 years!

The Palais Royal district was a popular quarter in pre-Revolutionary Paris. Diderot observed it in 1760:

> It is my practice to go, towards five o'clock in the evening, to take a turn in the Palais Royal. I am he whom you may see any afternoon sitting by myself and musing . . . . If the weather is too cold or too wet, I take shelter in the Regency coffee-house. There I amuse myself by looking on while they play chess. Nowhere in the world do they play chess as skilfully as in Paris, and nowhere in Paris as they do at this coffee-house . . .

The **Café Procope** had been founded across the street from the Comédie Française, a location bound to appeal to the actors and audience of the most famous theater in Paris. There's a story about the Procope and Voltaire. Apparently the great writer wanted to know what the public was saying about his new tragedy, *Semiramis*, produced in 1748. A friend of his wrote:

> It appeared to him that he could nowhere learn it better than in the Café de Procope, which was also called the Antre [cavern] de Procope, because it was very dark even in full day, and ill lighted in the evenings . . . . Monsieur de Voltaire wished to appear there, but in disguise and altogether incognito . . . On the second night of "Semiramis" he borrowed a clergyman's clothes: dressed himself in cassock and long cloak; black stockings, girdle, bands, breviary itself; nothing was forgotten. He clapped on a large peruke [wig] unpowdered,

very ill combed, which covered more than half of his cheeks and left nothing to be seen but the end of a long nose . . . . In this equipment, then, the author of "Semiramis" proceeded on foot to the Café Procope, where he squatted himself in a corner; and waiting for the end of the play, called for a bavaroise, a small roll of bread, and the *Gazette*. It was not long till those familiars of the Parterre and tenants of the café stept in. They instantly began discussing the new tragedy. Its partisans and its adversaries pleaded their cause with warmth; each giving his reasons . . . . During all this time, Monsieur de Voltaire, with spectacles on nose, head stooping over the *Gazette* which he pretended to be reading, was listening to the debate; profiting very much by reasonable observations, suffering very much to hear very absurd ones and not answer them, which irritated him.

Before the French Revolution there were 600 to 700 cafés in Paris. Those near the Palais Royal were particularly important as meeting places for politicians. Some of the cafés on the Right Bank were frequented by the leaders of the Reign of Terror. Robespierre was said to be a regular chess player at the **Café de la Régence**. One day a young man came to his table and begged to be allowed to play chess. He managed to win two games. When asked what token of victory he wanted, the nervous young man turned out to be a woman whose fiancé had been condemned to death. Her mission had been to save him from the guillotine. Robespierre, generous for once, granted the pardon.

Writer Henry Shelley, in *Old Paris*, imagined what the **Café Procope** must have been like during the Reign of Terror:

As soon as the French Revolution broke out, the Café Procope seems to have attracted patrons of a different character. From about 1790 onwards the most conspicuous among its clients were the men who figured most prominently in that terrible upheaval. Here, then, drinking coffee or stronger beverages, or playing chess, or reading the newspapers, or engaging in animated debate, might have been seen Marat, with his large, bony face.... and Robespierre, with his projecting brow, his blue and deeply set eyes, his long lips ... and Danton, with his pock-marked face, terrible in its ugliness, and his piercing eyes.

Arthur Young, an English writer, was in Paris in 1789. He was astonished to observe how important cafés had become at the beginning of what was to become the French Revolution:

> The coffee-houses present yet more singular and astonishing spectacles; they are not only crowded within, but other expectant crowds are at the doors and windows, listening ... to certain orators, who from chairs or tables harangue each his little audience: the eagerness with which they are heard, and the thunder of applause they receive for every sentiment of more than common hardiness or violence against the present government, cannot easily be imagined.

After the Revolution, Napoleon was said to frequent the **Régence**. For many years his table was preserved as part of the café's history: Napoleon had spent hours there playing chess. Once, it was said, he arrived and found that he had forgotten his purse and was without any money. He had to leave his hat as a pledge of security until he could return to pay his bill.

The golden age of the café was in the nineteenth century. In 1841 there were about 4,000 cafés in Paris, led by the **Procope** and the **Régence**. The Régence was a meeting place for all of the literary men in Paris, including Voltaire and Rousseau. Jean-Jacques Rousseau would go there regularly, conspicuous in his fur cap and Armenian costume. Eventually the police had to be called in to control the large crowds that gathered to see the author of *Emile*.

Rousseau was also in the habit of frequenting the **Café Laurent**, a Right Bank café popular with literary men early in the eighteenth century. He made the mistake of circulating satiric verses aimed at many of the other regulars. His authorship was discovered, and after a quarrel he was turned out of the café.

The **Café de Paris**, formerly at 41 avenue de l'Opéra, with its famous regulars, was described by Francis Carco:

> The Café de Paris occupied the building which forms the angle of the Boulevard and the rue Taitbout. "You reached the *grands salons* of the ground floor," recalls one of those who frequented it, "by a flight of several steps, similar to the one at Tortoni's."
>
> Musset, Balzac, and Alexandre Dumas used to go there to enjoy casseroled veal, which, they claimed, could not really be appreciated anywhere else . . . . It was while he was passing this establishment . . . that Mery bumped into Balzac and asked him what brought him to these parts on his own. Balzac was wearing dress trousers and a frock coat with velvet lapels. Immediately pulling out of his pocket an almanac which noted that sunrise was at 4:45, he replied: "I'm being pursued by bailiffs and forced to hide during the day . . . but at this hour they can't arrest me, so I walk."

In 1857, according to the brothers Goncourt, the **Café Riche** was "a headquarters of those men of letters who wear gloves." The Goncourts left a memorable description of the Riche's clientele, which included the poet Baudelaire:

> At the entrance, in the room separated from ours by two pillars, you can see here and there a few ears pricked up and drinking in the talk of our circle . . . dandies frittering away the last of their little fortune, or young men from the Stock Exchange, Rothschild's clerks, who have brought along some high grade tart from the Cirque or Mabille . . . .

Baudelaire had supper at the table next to ours. He was without a cravat, his shirt open at the neck and his head shaved, just as if he were going to be guillotined. A single affectation: his little hands were washed and cared for, the nails kept scrupulously clean. The face of a maniac, a voice that cuts like a knife, and a precise elocution that tries to copy Saint-Just and succeeds. He denies, with some obstinacy and a certain harsh anger, that he has offended morality with his verse.

In the 1890s, the **Napolitain Café** was favored by leading boulevardiers, dramatic critics, and several famous writers, including Guy de Maupassant. Actress and writer Cornelia Otis Skinner mentioned another habitué: "And there would occasionally come in, brought by her overbearing husband, a shy, wide-eyed girl who also wrote books, but nobody knew it then because the books were all signed by the name of her overbearing husband. Eventually she was to sign her own name to those enchanting works and the name she signed was Colette."

The **Café Procope** was one of the poet Paul Verlaine's favorite haunts. As Henry Shelley told it: "Verlaine preempted Voltaire's table and seat and held his court in the tiny saloon at the rear of the café. The poet of decadence had many followers, and his advent at the Procope meant a large addition to the customers of the hour . . ." Shelley confidently predicted the rapid demise of the Procope: "That was the last flicker of the famous café."

Guillaume Apollinaire left a lively account of the café scene in Montparnasse just before World War I in an article published in *Le Mercure de France*:

Montparnasse, according to anyone who lives in the surrounding quarters, is a quarter of crackpots . . . . At the angle of boulevard du Montparnasse and rue Delambre: Le Dôme—a steady clientele of rich people, aestheticians from Massachussets or from the banks of the Spree . . . it is here that one decides which of the French painters will be admired in Germany.

.... Further off, to the right on boulevard Raspail, the small Café des Vigourelles shelters many frisky young people on the days when there's no dancing at the Bal Bullier.

.... In the streets around the Montparnasse cemetery are the homes of famous former inhabitants of Montmartre, many of them like Picasso lived in the well-known house of 13 rue Ravignan. While it has a different local color than the Montmartre of before, Montparnasse today is no less gay, simple and easy-going.

.... Very soon I bet Montparnasse will alas have its night-clubs, its cabaret-singers just as it has its painters and its poets. The day some Bruant will celebrate in his songs the various spots of this quarter so full of fantasy...

What is left of the famous historic cafés? The oldest of them all, the one frequented by Voltaire and Verlaine, is still open:

The **Café Procope**, 13 rue de l'Ancienne Comédie, 75006 Paris (43.26.99.20). Métro: Odéon. The Procope was restored for the Bicentennial of the Revolution. Menus begin at about 99 francs. Coffee is available for 15 francs in the café-bar section from 11 a.m. to 1 a.m.

In the same area, and less expensive:

Relais Odéon, 132 boulevard Saint-Germain, 75006 Paris (43.29.81.80). Métro: Odéon. A *brasserie* since 1900, the Relais has still retained some of its Belle Epoque charm, and charges only 5.50 and 12 francs for coffee, 10 and 19 for beer, 10.50 and 18.20 for juice and soda, and 14 or 18 francs for a sandwich. It has an entrance in the same passage as the Café Procope, and is conveniently opposite the statue of Danton and the métro Odéon.

Le Mazet, 61 rue Saint-André-des-Arts, 75006 Paris (43.54.68.81). Métro: Odéon. People from all over—including France—have written enthusiastic comments in several languages

about the welcome they've received here. They send back
invitations and memorabilia to Pierrot and Pauline, the genial
proprietors of this lively, friendly bistro. Coffee is 5.50 and 10
francs, sandwiches 15 francs and up.

The **Café de Paris** no longer exists, but you can see one of
its elegant Art Nouveau rooms in the Musée Carnavelet, at the
corner of the rue Payenne and the rue des Francs Bourgeois in
the Marais. Formerly the Paris residence of Madame de Sévigné,
the Carnavalet also houses a stunning turn-of-the-century jewelry
shop, Fouquet's—designed by Alphonse Mucha—and the bed
room of Marcel Proust, lined with cork to keep out sound.

Less historic, but useful if you happen to be in the area are:
Au Cour Couronné, 6 rue de la Ferronnerie, 75001 Paris
(45.08.11.15). Métro: Châtelet. This brasserie and tearoom has
a view of the Place des Innocents. In cream and green, with
wood paneling, **Au Cour** keeps prices reasonable for this area: coffee 10 francs, tea or Coke 21, beer 16 francs and up, wine
17 and up, a croissant 8 francs and a sandwich 15.

Le Caveau Montpensier, 15 rue Montpensier, 75001 Paris.
Métro: Palais-Royal. A variety of beers is available here.

In the Comédie Française area:

Le Nemours, 2 Galerie de Nemours, 75001 Paris
(42.61.34.14). Imposing pillars, wicker chairs, and a view of
the Comédie Française! All come with coffee at 12 francs. An
intellectual crowd—you see several *Le Mondes* unfolded, with
a few *Le Figaros* thrown in. Elegant without being really
expensive.

At **Café Jean Nicot**, 173 rue Saint-Honoré, 75001 Paris
(42.60.49.77). You may enjoy the neon signs and mural in
honor of Jean Nicot, the diplomat who introduced tobacco to
France.

Chartier, 7 rue du Faubourg Montmartre, 75009 Paris
(47.70.86.29). A restaurant, Chartier is open daily. An
old standby. Lunch or dinner from about 70 francs. The
house red wine is often better than some of the named

varieties. Look around and appreciate the turn-of-the-century decor.

Chez Léon (Le Rubis), 10 rue du Marché-Saint-Honoré, 75001 Paris (42.61.03.34). Métro: Pyramides or Palais-Royal. Open from 7 a.m. to 10 p.m., this is an authentic bistro between the Tuileries and the Opéra, where low-priced lunches and a good range of wines by the glass are available. Sandwiches are made with poilâne bread.

L'Entracte, Bar de, 47 rue Montpensier, 75001 Paris (42.97.57.76). Métro: Palais-Royal. Diderot was one of the habitués of a café on the same location with a different name. Now frequented by actors from the *Comédie Française* and the *Théâtre du Palais Royal.*

Terrasse de la Samaritaine, 19 rue de la Monnaie, 75001 Paris (40.41.20.20). Métro: Pont-Neuf. Lunch with a view from the top of this department store–prices are reasonable too! Coffee is 10 francs.

Willi's Wine Bar, 13 rue des Petits-Champs, 75001 Paris (42.61.05.09). Métro: Palais-Royal. One of the best-known wine bars in the city, run by an Englishman who knows his wines, Willi's is fairly expensive.

Voltaire, Le, 27 quai Voltaire, 75007 Paris (42.61.17.49). Formerly a café, now a restaurant beside the Seine, Voltaire is famous as the place where Baudelaire wrote Les Fleurs du Mal. Francophiles will like its proximity to the Documentation Française, an excellent resource on Paris, France, and the French.

Zimmer, 1 place du Châtelet, 75001 Paris (42.38.74.03). Métro: Châtelet. Convenient to the theaters, the Zimmer gives you an outstanding view of the Place du Châtelet and the Seine.

3
Modern French Writers:
The Left Bank

"There is only one trait that marks the writer. He is always watching. It's a kind of trick of the mind and he is born with it."—Morley Callaghan

During the 1930s, certain cafés on the Left Bank of the Seine were the regular haunts of French writers who have since become famous, notably Jean-Paul Sartre and Simone de Beauvoir. Sartre, through his extraordinary literary output—articles, plays, and novels—made Existentialism accessible to ordinary people. De Beauvoir, his lifelong companion and intellectual equal, was to write *The Second Sex*, as well as novels and the books of memoirs which remain the best record of their life together. Sartre frequented first the **Dôme**, and later the **Café de Flore**. He told why he decided to abandon the Dôme:

From 1930 to 1939 I went regularly to the Dôme in Montparnasse. As I was a teacher and hadn't much money,

27

I lived in a hotel; and like all people who live in hotels, I spent most of the day in cafés. In 1940 the "regulars" of the Dôme began to go elsewhere, for two reasons: the Métro station "Vavin" was closed, and we had to make our way to the Dôme in the evenings, in complete darkness and on foot from the Gare Montparnasse. Besides, the Dôme was overrun with Germans, and these Germans were tactless enough to bring their own tea and coffee, and to have these prepared and served in front of us Frenchmen, who were already reduced to drinking some anonymous and ghastly substitute.

The fortunes of the Café de Flore ... were made by the fact that it was just across the road from the station of Saint-Germain-des-Prés. It had previously been merely an annex of the Deux Magots, but in 1939 or thereabouts, Picasso, Léon-Paul Fargue, and André Breton began to go to the Flore. A lot of cinema people followed their example, and a lot of successful painters and celebrities of one sort or another. I was only a shabby little teacher at that time and I was too shy to go in.

In her memoirs of the 1930s and the war years, Simone de Beauvoir said that before the war she was an ostrich: she tried to ignore politics and refused to admit what was happening. Still, she wrote of being "scared stiff" by events in Germany, particularly by the pact between Hitler and Mussolini and the invasion of Austria. Later she described her attachment to the cafés when, in 1939, with Sartre having left for the army and war imminent, she was alone in Paris. She would get up at 3 in the morning and go down to the **Café du Dôme**:

The Dôme is noisy; lots of uniforms. Out on the *terrasse* two tarts are sitting with their arms around a couple of officers. One of the girls is singing, as though from sheer habit. The officers take no notice of them. Loud shouts and laughter from inside.

Five days later, De Beauvoir was to note in her journal:

> I have a close and affectionate regard for this little Montparnasse square. I love its half-empty sidewalk cafés .... I feel part of the family, as it were, and that protects me against depression.

After the German forces arrived and occupied Paris in 1940, De Beauvoir returned from a brief flight to the country, hoping to be able to take up her life as a philosophy teacher at the Lycée Camille-Sée. Once more she found comfort in leaving her tiny room for the better ambiance of a café:

> It's lovely weather. I resume my usual place at the Dôme .... Almost no one about on the boulevard. Two trucks full of young Germans in gray go past; this has become so common a sight that now it hardly strikes me as odd.

At about the same time, A.J. Leibling, correspondent for the *New Yorker*, wrote that he could judge the morale of Parisians early in World War II by the appearance of people he observed in cafés:

> I can't remember exactly when I first became frightened, or when I first began to notice that the shapes of people's faces were changing. There was plenty of food in Paris. People got thin worrying. I think I noticed first the thinning faces of the sporting girls in the cafés. Since the same girls came to the same cafés every night, it was easy to keep track.

"Paris is now the capital of limbo."—Janet Flanner, in "Paris Germany," *New Yorker*, Dec. 7, 1940

Word reached Simone de Beauvoir that Sartre had been taken prisoner on June 21 in 1940. She recorded in her diary that the only thing that interested her was the date of his release. In May, after the German invasion of Holland and Belgium, Sartre had written in an optimistic mood, saying that the Germans could not defend such a vast front. The German army had continued its advance. Despite the chaos to which life had been reduced, Sartre still managed to continue working on a novel. For relaxation, he would play chess. There were 10 days of retreating—then Sartre's unit was taken prisoner in Alsace.

Even though he was a prisoner of war in a remote part of France, Sartre's life continued to be affected by the time he had spent in Paris cafés. One day another prisoner, observing Sartre's haggard and unshaven condition, asked if by any chance he was related to the intellectual who used to frequent the **Flore**. Soon after that Sartre began to shave and clean up. Shortly after his capture, De Beauvoir received a penciled note from Sartre himself, saying that he was not being badly treated and might soon be home.

At the beginning of the new school year, De Beauvoir and all of the other employees at her *lycée* were forced to sign documents affirming that they were neither Freemasons nor Jews. She found this "repugnant," but decided that there was no alternative but to sign. The cafés helped her to get through the winter:

> That winter was even colder than the previous one . . . . There was a shortage of coal, and my room was not heated . . . . I would hurry over to the Dôme in search of a little warmth; the place was no longer out of bounds to the Germans, and while I gulped down my ersatz coffee, various "gray mice" [German soldiers] would be putting out butter and jam on their tables . . . . As in the old days, I used to work in one of the booths at the back . . . . Most evenings I spent in the Flore, where no member of the Occupation forces ever set foot.

When, after months of captivity, Sartre managed to escape, his first meeting with De Beauvoir was at the **Café des Trois**

Mousquetaires. Sartre explained to the surprised De Beauvoir that since the prison camp was close to the Luxembourg border, his escape had been relatively easy. He came back to Paris determined not to make any compromises with the enemy, not even to buy food on the black market. He was anxious to organize a resistance movement. As De Beauvoir told it:

> I went along with Sartre to one of these sessions, in the Closerie des Lilas .... All these groups had two things in common: a very limited effective strength, and an extraordinary lack of common caution .... We held our meetings in hotel rooms or someone's study at the Ecole Normale, where walls might well have ears.

After the Allied landing in North Africa on November 8, the winter was especially hard. One café, **Le Flore**, become particularly important to Beauvoir and Sartre:

> At the Flore, at least, it wasn't cold .... It was during this time that we got into the habit of spending all our leisure time in the Flore: and not only because we found it offered us comparative comfort. It was our own special resort. We felt at home there; it sheltered us from the outside world.

Most people concentrated their attention on the problem of food. In July of 1941, an article in *La Gerbe* chronicled the difficulty of finding enough to eat in Paris:

> Eating, and more important, eating well, is the theme song of Paris life. In the street, in the métro, in drawing rooms, in cafés, all you hear about is food: how to track down some skinny bird or anaemic lobster like an Indian scout; how to arrange a genuine prewar meal (don't breathe a word!). At the theater or movies, when there's an old play or movie with a huge banquet scene, the audience breaks into delirious cries of joy.

Another reporter for *La Gerbe* described an experience in a café on the rue Lafayette in November of the same year:

> It was noon. The bar was packed. Five minutes earlier, there had been only a few thirsty gossipers sampling high-powered rumors and low-powered drinks. They were swept aside by crowds from nearby shops and offices, mostly women and young men. Two of the women, next to me, ordered Viandox* . . . . Others were drinking a yellowish coffee . . . . All of them opened their bags and took out small pieces of bread which they began to eat.
>
> I offered a drink to the women next to me. But they hesitated.
>
> "It makes your head spin," said one of them eventually.
>
> The other said, "And besides, it might make you hungry."
>
> They then took two more Viandox. So deciding to go the whole way, I offered them a couple of crackers. Then the first one said solemnly and contentedly, without so much as the flicker of a smile: "Good lunch we had today."

Even in the home-like setting of her favorite café, the **Flore**, Simone de Beauvoir knew there were collaborators around. Two journalists would come in daily at ten in the morning and loudly make their collaborationist, anti-Semitic views known. They were the exception. Most customers of the Flore "were firmly opposed both to Fascism and to collaboration, and made no secret of it," according to De Beauvoir. Later in the day the room would fill up, and De Beauvoir recorded that by *apéritif* time it was full:

> You would see Picasso there, smiling at Dora Marr . . . and Jacques Prévert holding forth to a circle of acquaintances

---

* Viandox was a beef consommé. It was inexpensive and used for giving a feeling of temporary fullness.

. . . . I went out for dinner, and then returned again till closing time. It always gave me a thrill of pleasure at night to walk in out of the icy darkness and find myself in this warm, well lit, snug retreat, with its charming blue and red wallpaper.

At the **Flore** De Beauvoir met several other famous writers. She first encountered Albert Camus there while she was sitting at her usual table with Jean-Paul Sartre. As she described the meeting, the author of *The Stranger* turned out to be "crazy about the theatre," and Sartre just happened to be working on a new play. So the ice was quickly broken.

In May 1944, while sitting at the **Flore** they happened to meet an unknown poet whom Jean Cocteau had "discovered." It was none other than Jean Genêt, the notorious thief who was later to write several highly controversial plays. De Beauvoir met him at the Flore when she was sitting there with Sartre and Camus. She was struck by his brusque behavior, and said that Genêt seemed to be "a pretty hard case."

Yet De Beauvoir and Sartre were won over by Genêt: "He . . . asserted that he would never hesitate to rob or betray a friend; yet I never heard him speak ill of anyone."

When the fame of Sartre and De Beauvoir began to interfere seriously with their work, they found it necessary to leave their usual hangouts, the **Flore**, the **Lipp**, and the **Deux Magots**. They began to frequent the bar in the basement of the Hotel du Pont-Royal. It was there in 1949 that they saw Truman Capote, whom De Beauvoir remembered as looking like "a white mushroom" in his large white sweater. She remarked on his fastidiousness and on her surprise that he was even smaller than Sartre. Capote got his revenge later on. In a description of the two in *Answered Prayers,* he described Sartre as "pipe-sucking and pasty-hued" as he sat with De Beauvoir, "his spinsterish moll." Actually, De Beauvoir was considered attractive by people who knew her, although she usually paid little attention to fashion.

A favorite with Left Bank writers was the **Brasserie Lipp**. In *Force of Circumstance*, De Beauvoir often mentions going there to have lunch with Sartre. The *brasserie* was also patronized by Picasso, De Gaulle, and a number of famous writers, including James Joyce.

After the Liberation, De Beauvoir kept on going to the cafés which had become a second home to her. She described the conception of *The Second Sex*; she had finished an essay, and was wondering what to do next:

> I sat in the Deux Magots and gazed at the blank sheet of paper .... I felt the need to write in my fingertips .... In fact, I wanted to write about myself .... I realized that the first question to come up was: What has it meant to me to be a woman?

The French writers who founded the surrealist movement used to meet at **Les Deux Magots**. Here Louis Aragon, André Breton, and Philippe Soupault put together the *Surrealist Manifestos* in the late 1920s. As Janet Flanner wrote:

> The surrealists had their own club table facing the door of the Deux Magots, from which vantage point a seated surrealist could conveniently insult any newcomer with whom he happened to be feuding, or discuss his plan to horsewhip an editor of some belligerent and anti-surrealist newspaper for having mentioned his name or, worse, for having failed to mention it ...

Other surrealists who would drop by included Max Ernst, Man Ray, and Joan Miró.

Where are the historic meeting places of the French intelligentsia? They are relatively easy to find, and tend to be grouped in the Montparnasse area of the Left Bank:

Closerie des Lilas, 171 boulevard du Montparnasse, 75006 Paris (43.26.70.50). Métro: Port-Royal. Like the famous **Deux Magots,** the Closerie was as important to American writers in Paris as to the French. For this reason, both cafés have already been described in the chapter "American Cafés." (See pp.12–13.)

Le Flore, 172 boulevard Saint-Germain, 75006 Paris (45.48.55.26). Métro: Saint-Germain-des-Prés. Le Flore is where Simone de Beauvoir and Jean-Paul Sartre spent much of their time in the 1930s and 1940s. Here De Beauvoir did a considerable amount of writing her own works and editing those of Sartre—during the war and afterwards. Sartre is remembered as one of the worst customers: "He would never order a second drink," reported Pierre Boubal, the proprietor who remembers him. Other regulars included Camus, Jacques Prévert, and Marcel Carné. Le Flore is right next to Les Deux Magots, important in the 1920s as an "American" café. The Flore is open from 7:30 a.m. to 1:30 a.m. A continental breakfast here is about 40 francs, and coffee alone, 21.

Le Café du Dôme, 108 boulevard du Montparnasse, 75014 Paris (43.35.25.81). Métro: Vavin. Open between 10 a.m. and 12:45 a.m., the Dôme has become an expensive restaurant. Still, coffee at the bar is a reasonable 8 francs, and if you sit down, 15. Service is friendly. There is a zinc bar, and the air conditioning can be welcome on a hot summer day. The walls are enameled in a darker shade of the famous Hermès orange.

Brasserie Lipp, 151 boulevard Saint-Germain, 75006 Paris (45.48.53.91). Métro: Saint-Germain-des-Prés. An elegant, turn-of-the-century *brasserie.* The house speciality is *choucroute*—sauerkraut, served with pork. Open from 8 a.m. to 1 a.m. Full meals around 300 francs, but coffee or beer is still only 18 francs—more reasonable than at either the **Deux Magots** or the **Café de Flore** across the street. Closed mid-July to mid-August.

Today's writers frequent:
Café de la Mairie, 8 Place Saint-Sulpice, 75006 Paris

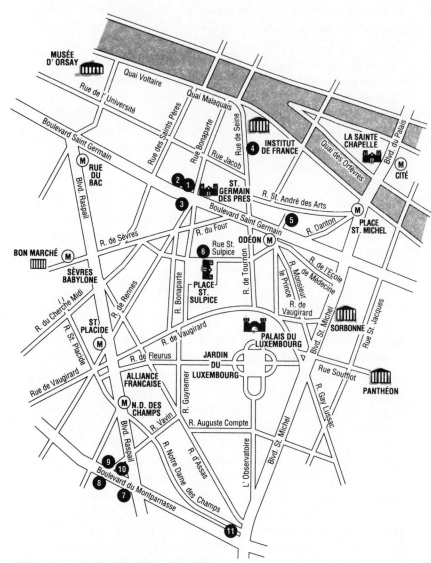

Writers' and Artists' Cafés: Left Bank

1. Les Deux Magots, 6 Place St.-Germain
2. Le Flore, 172 bd. St.-Germain
3. Brasserie Lipp, 151 bd. St.-Germain
4. La Palette, 43 rue de Seine
5. Le Procope, 13 rue de L' Ancienne Comédie
6. Café de la Mairie, 8 Place St.-Sulpice
7. Le Dôme, 108 bd. du Montparnasse
8. La Coupole, 102 bd. du Montparnasse
9. Le Sélect, 99 bd. du Montparnasse
10. La Rotonde, 105 bd. du Montparnasse
11. La Closerie des Lilas, 171 bd. du Montparnasse

(43.26.67.82). Métro: Saint-Sulpice. "Though only a café, the Café de la Mairie served food and drinks to Hemingway, Fitzgerald, Djuna Barnes, Samuel Beckett, and numerous other writers then and now," wrote Noel Riley Fitch in *Walks in Hemingway's Paris*. Coffee is 5.60 and 11.50 francs.

Fouquet's, 99 avenue des Champs-Elysées, 75008 Paris (47.23.70.60). Métro: Georges-V. Open daily until 1:30 a.m. André Bazan, a writer for *L'Express Paris*, described the pre-dinner drink scene at Fouquet's as "elegant." He also remarked: "Here around 8:00 p.m. one can still encounter several old writers still persevering," and said that around the tables placed a good distance apart, people taste the drink of their choice— notably a *kir*, at 38 francs, or an *apéritif* at 44. (A *kir* is a mixture of dry white wine and *crème de cassis*, blackcurrant liqueur).

Aux Négociants, 27 rue Lambert, 75018 Paris (46.06.15.11). Métro: Château-Rouge. Open daily except for weekends and in August. Poet Dominique Joubert, interviewed in *Le Quotidien de Paris*, mentioned Aux Négociants as a café favored by poets as well as by working people from Montmartre. (See also description page 75). A full meal costs about 180 francs, with coffee only 5.50 and 9 francs.

Le Vaudeville, 29 rue Vivienne, 75002 Paris (40.20.04.62). Métro: Bourse. Situated opposite the Bourse, Le Vaudeville is a lively café-brasserie-restaurant, frequented not only by stock-brokers from the Bourse, but also by writers for Agence France Presse, on the same square. Coffee 5.50 and 8 francs.

Le Christine, 1 rue Christine, 75006 Paris (40.51.71.64). Métro: Odéon. Le Christine is now more an attractive wine bar and restaurant than a café. Coffee is 12 francs, wines 15 francs and up. Gertrude Stein and Alice B. Toklas lived nearby at 5 rue Christine from 1938 to 1946, after moving from the rue de Fleurus. Le Christine is patronized these days by writers from the magazine *L'Evénement du jeudi* across the street.

37

The Cafés of Paris

Bar du Pont Royal, 7 rue Montalembert, 75007 Paris (45.44.38.27). Métro: rue du Bac. Once a refuge for Sartre and Simone de Beauvoir when they had become too well known to be left undisturbed at their favorite cafés, now the Bar du Pont Royal is frequented by writers from Gallimard Press.

Guinness Tavern, 31 bis, rue des Lombards, 75001 Paris (42.33.26.45). Métro: Châtelet. Open all night until 6 a.m., the Guinness Tavern is patronized by journalists in the early hours of the morning. Reasonable bar prices: coffee 5 francs, beer 14, juice and soda 7. When there is live music, a 60 franc *consommation* is required.

Several reliable cafés are clustered near the large building on the rue Montmartre housing the newspaper and magazine *Le Figaro*. Its writers can choose from:

Le Brazza, at 86 rue Montmartre, 75002 Paris. Métro: Sentier. Here coffee is 5.20 and 8.50 francs, hot chocolate 6.50 and 10, tea 8.50 and 12, beer 5.50 and 8.50, and wine 6.50 and 8.50.

Le Paris-Montmartre, 106 rue Montmartre, 75002 Paris (42.33.17.13). Métro: Châtelet-Les Halles. Coffee is 5 and 8 francs, beer 9 and 12, juice 13 and 16, and a sandwich 13 and 15.

Paris Bar, 98 rue Montmartre, 75002 Paris (42.36.40.28). Métro: Châtelet-Les Halles. This is a small, enticing hangout, long, narrow, and resembling a railway car. Coffee 5 and 7 francs.

Le Tambour, 41 rue Montmartre, 75002 Paris (42.33.06.90). Métro: Châtelet-Les Halles or Sentier. Le Tambour is striking, with a deep green façade, a bar in brass and burgundy, and framed photos of old Paris on cream-colored walls. Here the ambiance and service are particularly impressive. Coffee is 5.50 and 8 francs.

4

Maigret's Cafés: From the République to the Bastille, with a Look at the Marais and the Place des Vosges

"From his office window he could see a stretch of the Seine, the Place Saint-Michel, and a floating wash house, all shrouded in a blue haze through which the gas lamps twinkled like stars as they lit up one by one."—Maigret's view from 36 quai des Orfévres

Inspector Maigret is a gourmet—no doubt about that. Enthusiasts of the great detective created by Georges Simenon have followed their hero in spirit into many a café or *brasserie* where Maigret would stop to quench his thirst with a glass of wine or an *apéritif*, or to savor a meal. Sometimes cafés become central to the plots in Maigret's investigations.

In 1929 an unknown young writer who had been using the pseudonym "Georges Sim" left Paris for a tour of the European canals. During the trip, a stopover in the Netherlands was necessary when the boat he was travelling on had to be recaulked. The work made so much noise that he was forced to get off to find a quiet place to write. He found an old abandoned barge. Installing a large packing case as a typing table, he started to write the first mystery featuring Inspector Maigret. Simenon visualized Maigret as a large, powerful man:

> He had neither moustache nor heavy boots, his suit was of quite good material and cut . . . . but his frame was plebian . . . huge and bony. Strong muscles swelled beneath his jacket . . . . He had a characteristic stance, too . . . . It expressed something more than self-confidence, and yet it was not conceit . . .

Simenon had the brilliant idea of launching a series of the Maigret mysteries with a ball at the Boule Blanche, a night-club in Montparnasse. Invitations looked like police summonses. All of the guests were fingerprinted when they arrived, and the room was decorated with crime-related objects—handcuffs, police belts, and so on. The ball was a great success. With the importance that cafés and bars were to assume in the mysteries, it seems fitting that a famous café, the **Coupole**, had to be opened at 1 a.m. to replenish the depleted stocks of whiskey and champagne.

The typical Paris café scene appears again and again in Simenon's pages. Nowhere is café life brought out better than in *Maigret et son mort (Maigret's Dead Man)*. In this story, Inspector Maigret is trying to find out who murdered a young man and dumped his body on the Place de la Concorde. Maigret feels strongly involved in this case because the murder victim had made frantic appeals to him for help, saying that he was being pursued by people who were out to get him. Each time he had telephoned from a different café. The cafés were not far from Maigret's own neighborhood near the Place de la République.

Trying to learn the identity of the murderer, Maigret reasons that the victim must himself have had something to do with a café. He notes that at each café where the murdered man had stopped to telephone for help from his pursuers, he ordered a *suze*, a bitter drink with a low alcohol content. This is just the type of drink that somebody might order if for reasons of work he had to accept rounds of drinks without losing his sobriety.

Maigret has to explain to his supervisor, a younger man who seems to have no common sense or real knowledge of Paris, that the victim was almost certainly *dans la limonade*, a slang term meaning that he was involved in the café trade, whether as a waiter, barman, dishwasher, or proprietor. He points out certain characteristics that these people all share:

> Look at their feet. They wear fine, supple shoes, almost slippers. You will never see a waiter or a maître d' wearing thick-soled sports shoes. And they're used to wearing white shirts because of their profession.

Maigret already knows the interests of most waiters: " . . . waiters have a strong taste for horseracing and many of them who work early in the morning, or at night, spend much of their spare time at the races."

In the course of the case, Maigret studies little neighborhood bars and cafés. A few customers eat there regularly, at a table without a tablecloth. Generally the boss's wife does the cooking, and only the day's special or *plat du jour* is available. Later Maigret realizes that the victim must have come from the area between the Bastille and the Hôtel de Ville, not far from his own neighborhood, since his appeals for help came from that area: "Parisians are fiercely attached to their own districts," he observes, "feeling that that is the only place where they are really safe."

Finally Maigret finds the café that must have belonged to the murdered man. It is an unusual little place for Paris, situated on a corner, only one story high, with a red tiled roof and yellow walls. Large letters announce the name: "Chez Petit Albert." Maigret finds this café absolutely typical of a rural café, the sort of place that could be found in almost any village in France.

A sting operation is set up, with a couple hired to take the place of Albert and his wife, who are said to be on vacation. Maigret stays around, playing the role of a member of the family. He even joins spontaneously in conversations among the regulars.

Looking for someone else who might have known the murdered man, Maigret goes to a *brasserie*. Here he chats with the former owner, who goes into detail about the qualities of an ideal waiter:

What matters most in our business is cheerfulness. People who go to cafés like to see smiling faces. I remember one waiter, for instance, very decent, who had I don't know how many children, who used to bend over customers ordering soda water or Vichy or anything non-alcoholic, and whisper confidentially, "Have you got an ulcer too?" . . . He talked of nothing else, and I had to fire him because people used to move away when they saw him coming towards their table.

In what *brasserie* might Maigret have heard this? Probably in one of the many clustered on the Place de la République, close to his own apartment on the boulevard Richard-Lenoir. Two stand out:

Le Relais d'Eguisheim, 6 Place de la République, 75011 Paris (47.00.44.10). A one-plate meal or *plat* is available at 55, 65, or 75 francs. You can get coffee for 13 francs or beer for 21.

Le Thermomètre, its neighbor right next door at 4 Place de la République, (47.00.30.78). Here the prices are similar. The ambiance is more sober, but you may appreciate the classy look of its wood-panelled interior.

Cafés are central to the plot of *Maigret et le voleur paresseux (Maigret and the Lazy Burglar)*. A man has been murdered and his face rendered unrecognizable, probably by blows struck after he was already dead. Yet Maigret has a feeling that he knew the victim. Tattoos and fingerprints prove that Maigret's first hunch was right: the murdered man was someone he knew, one Cuendet, a professional thief who had moved to Paris years ago from Switzerland. Cuendet had found a means of using cafés in his work:

He had become a sudden and temporary habitué of various local cafés.

A quiet man, who used to sit for hours in his favorite corner . . . watching the scene outside . . . . So that after a time a whole block of apartments would have revealed their every secret.

He was capable of sitting for hours in some café . . . [with] white wine in front of him . . . . His needs were very few. But the list of jewels he had stolen . . . represented a fortune.

At the same time that he is investigating the death of Cuendet, Maigret learns of a gang of thieves who have been using a café as a headquarters from which to organize their holdups. The examining magistrate, Cajou, insists that this is the case Maigret should concentrate on. Cuendet was a nobody—his death could have been a settling of accounts in the underworld. Irritated that he is being directed by someone who knows next to nothing about what his job involves, Maigret continues to pursue both cases.

A breakthrough in the case of the holdups begins with the background work of one of his policemen. Inspector Nicholas reports on his observations in a café. He relates that he had watched René Lussac, who worked for a firm of musical instrument makers. Lussac went regularly to the **Café des Amis**, at the Porte de Versailles:

Two men were waiting for him, and they began to play belote, like people who are in the habit of meeting round the same table.

Nicolas wondered what Lussac was doing there and why the men had picked such an unappealing café for their card game.

. . . At precisely half past nine Lussac went to the cash-desk and bought a counter for the automatic telephone . . .

It does not take Maigret long to determine that the leader of the gang is a man named Fernand, who gives regular instructions to his accomplices by telephone from the Café des Amis.

Before the case can be solved, a police raid is necessary at the café. But more important for Maigret is his own continuing private investigation into the life of Cuendet and his dependants. His concern about the dead criminal shows up the difference between the examining magistrate and himself:

The whole subject had apparently been dismissed. Cajou, the examining magistrate, felt sure he need give no more thought to it.

He had settled the question in his own mind the very first day:

Vendetta in the underworld . . .

Cajou didn't know old Justine [Cuendet's mother] or the little flat in the Rue Mouffetard . . .

In this mystery, Georges Simenon displays his characteristic awareness of the small details, the insider information that makes it possible for the reader to experience the ambiance of a neighborhood, the feelings evoked by a time of year, and the sense of being in a small café.

Here are some cafés and bistros not far from Maigret's apartment on the boulevard Richard-Lenoir or within his reach—from the **République** to the **Bastille**, including the **Marais**:

Ange'vin, a great bistro, formerly at 24 rue Richard Lenoir, has been moved to 168 rue Montmartre. Métro: Bourse or Rue Montmartre. You could imagine Maigret at a table in this bistro recalling Paris in the 1950s. The Richard Lenoir Ange'vin had the homey ambiance of the ideal neighborhood bistro, with the day's specials chalked up on slate boards above the highly original bar. I have no doubt that Ange'vin in its new location, presided over by the same genial host, Jean-Pierre Robinot, will achieve the same high levels for food, wine, and hospitality as the original. Worth a visit. Full meals, 170 to 200 francs.

Still in Maigret's neighborhood, **Le Paris**, at 24 boulevard Richard-Lenoir, on the corner of the boulevard Richard-Lenoir and the rue Saint-Sabin, 75011 Paris (47.00.87.47). Métro: Bréguet-Sabin. Here is an old fashioned zinc bar and good ambiance. Prices are reasonable too: coffee 5.30 and 10, tea 13 and 17, Coke 14 and 18, wine 6 and 11 francs, and beer 9.60 and 16 francs.

The Clown Bar, 114 rue Amelot, Paris 75011 (43.55.87.35). Métro: Filles du Calvaire. Open noon to 3:30 p.m. and 6:30 to 1 a.m., the Clown Bar is closed Sundays and in August. You will pass this unusual bar on your way from the Place de la République to the Bastille. It is right off the boulevard du Temple and next to the spectacular Cirque d'Hiver (winter circus), built in 1852 and trimmed with fantastic bas-reliefs of circus performers and their horses. The Clown Bar also has a lively, colorful decor dating from 1919—well before Maigret's time—with charming murals of circus performers in original tiles. Wines by the glass start at 15 francs. The good food here is not cheap, but sandwiches are available for 25 francs. A lively, intellectual-looking crowd. Coffee can be had at the bar—after 10 p.m. the price rises to 12 francs.

Au Drapeau, 3 boulevard Beaumarchais, has been transformed into the **Flag Café**. Glossy paint and loud music have not improved the ambiance here, and it would be impossible to imagine Maigret in this changed setting. He'd be more at home at the nearby **Café des Phares**, 7 Place de la Bastille 75004 Paris (42.72.04.70), where coffee is 5 and 10 francs and people discuss philosophy on Sunday mornings.

Not far away, in the 11th arrondissement, close to the Bastille on the rue Saint-Sabin is a real find: the **Café de L'Industrie**, 16 rue Saint-Sabin, 75011 Paris (47.00.13.53). Métro: Bastille or Bréguet-Sabin. Here, in a café that looks as if it might have been Bogart's just before he went off to Casablanca, you can sip coffee for 5 francs standing or 9 seated at the dark red banquettes, or 9 and 14 after 10:00 p.m. Faded cream walls, the frosted Deco glass, old photos of French celebrities, Oriental rugs well past their first splendor, an artsy crowd, and strains of traditional French folksinging coming from the back create an ambiance of Old France. Lunch is around 50 francs.

Ma Bourgogne, at 19 Place des Vosges 75004 Paris (42.78.44.64) is really a restaurant—but coffee and other drinks are available during off-peak hours. This was the tabac mentioned in Simenon's *L'Amie de Madame Maigret*: "Everybody knew the square, with its three cafés: first the café-restaurant on the corner of the rue des Francs Bourgeois, then Le Grand Turenne opposite, and finally, 30 meters away, the Tabac des Vosges . . ." If you sit outside, you enjoy a view of the incomparable Place des Vosges: if indoors, you'll find the interior warm and welcoming, with dark oak beams. Coffee 6 and 14.

Convenient to the Musée Carnavelet is the **Café des Musées**, 49 rue de Turenne, 75003 Paris (42.72.96.17). This is a good stop for salads, sandwiches, and hot lunches. If you're a museum buff, another possibility is the café of the **Musée Picasso**, 5 rue Thorigny, in the same district and open to those who don't buy a museum ticket.

Le Béarn, a *brasserie* on the corner of the rue des Minimes and the rue de Béarn, near the Place des Vosges. Métro: Bastille or Chemin Vert. Here coffee is only 5.70 and 8.70 francs, beer 8 and 11, juice and soda 12.50 and 18.50, and sandwiches from 16. In this modern light wood and wicker setting, be prepared for light prices for food: omelettes are 18 francs and up and a cheese plate starts at 20.

Les Enfants Gâtés, 43 rue des Francs-Bourgeois, 75004 Paris (42.77.07.63). Métro: Saint-Paul. Coffee is 15 francs, a *café crème* 24, and pastry 30 francs. Open 11 to 7 daily, except in August.

Jacques Mélac, 42 rue Léon-Frot, 75011 Paris (43.70.59.27). Métro: Charonne. Open from 9 a.m. to 10:30 p.m. Closed weekends and in August. You can almost see Maigret standing here at the zinc bar. He wouldn't bother to glance at the jocular signs warning against drinking water: he would address his request to one of the young barmen coping with great slabs of cheese and *pain poilâne*, or perhaps to Jacques Mélac himself. They will cheerfully plop down a glass and a bottle with Mélac's own label on it in front of anyone who hesitates over the assortment available. The dark beams overhead, little tables outside, and the grapevines that curl over the doorway and wind along the roof give a feeling of country peacefulness to this place deep in Maigret's 11th district, off the usual tourist circuit. An impressive range of wines is available from 12 francs and up, as well as omelettes and a lunchtime *plat* for about 50 francs.

Baracane l'Oulette, 38 rue des Tournelles, 75004 Paris (42.71.43.33). Métro: Bastille. Near the Place des Vosges, where Maigret was sometimes called to investigate the murders of ambitious executives (*L'Ombre Chinois* is one such story). The food here shows the influence of the Bordeaux area; L'Oulette is more a restaurant than a café. Coffee and tea 14 and 16 francs.

Marais Plus, Le, 20 rue des Francs-Bourgeois, 75003 Paris (48.87.01.40). Métro: Saint-Paul. Open daily from 10 a.m. to 7:30 p.m., Marais Plus is a good place to stop in the Marais, and its prices are reasonable. Check "Country Cafés and *Salons de Thé*" for a more complete description (p. 105).

Café Martini, 11 rue du Pas de la Mule, 75004 Paris (42.77.05.04). Métro: Chemin Vert or Bastille. Here you are just off the Place des Vosges, yet enjoying low prices. This lively, cheerful café has an attractive old-style façade with its name in gold lettering. Coffee is 6 or 10 francs, depending on whether you sit or stand, and beer 12 or 15.

Le Temps des Cerises, 31 rue de la Cerisaie, 75004 Paris (42.72.08.63), near the Bastille. Métro: Bastille. Mentioned again in "Country Cafés" (see p. 104), Le Temps deserves a second look—it's small, charming, and friendly. This could have served as a model for the café Simenon describes as "Chez Petit Albert" in *Maigret et son mort*. Coffee is 6.70 and 9.50 francs. From 12 to 2 on weekdays, lunch is available for 68 francs.

Le Charbon, 109 rue Oberkampf 75011 Paris (43.57.55.13). Métro: Saint-Maur. Le Charbon charms the visitor by its turn-of-the-century decor. A mural high on the walls recalls Lautrec: dancers flaunt their crinolines under the watchful eyes of top-hatted gentlemen. Attracts a lively crowd, the young and the not-so-young. Coffee 6 and 10 francs. Open daily, 9:00 to 2:00 a.m.

La Perla, 26 rue François Miron, 75004 Paris (42.77.59.40). Métro: Hôtel de Ville. La Perla has a charming interior, with a long old-fashioned wood bar and old-fashioned chairs. It features Mexican food. Drink prices: coffee 12, *café crème* and tea 20, beer and wine 20 francs and up.

Chez Jojo, Le Natanya, 64 rue François Miron, 75004 Paris (48.04.36.09). This is a simple neighborhood café-restaurant just down the street from the one above. Here coffee is 6 and 7 francs, juice, soda and mineral water 15 and 17, and sandwiches 20 and 30. Closed in August.

Now, if you happen to be in the neighborhood of Maigret's office at **36 quai des Orfèvres**, near the Place Dauphine, here are some cafés you may want to try:

Bar du Caveau, 17 Place Dauphine, 75001 Paris (43.54.45.95).

Métro: Pont-Neuf. This café or bar is in the closest thing to a secret garden I've found in Paris. The Place Dauphine is behind Maigret's lair, the Police Judiciaire at 36 quai des Orfévres. It's near the Seine and next to several major tourist attractions— yet it has remained relatively undiscovered by outsiders. Here you can sit on a park bench enjoying the view, while outside the Place tourists are crossing the bridges, admiring Notre Dame, and trekking to La Sainte Chapelle. Once in a while one of the locals will emerge to walk a dog. At the Bar du Caveau, coffee is 12 francs, soda and juice 18, beer 15, mineral water 16, a wide selection of wines 12 francs and up, and sandwiches from 20 to 26 francs. The bar has a rustic look, with its beams and stone walls. Its location in the peaceful Place Dauphine doesn't hurt either. Open from 8:30 a.m. to 8 p.m. Closed weekends and December 15 to 31.

Les Deux Palais, 3 boulevard du Palais, 75004 Paris (43.54.20.86). Métro: Cité. Les Deux Palais is across the street from the Palais de Justice, near Maigret's office and the Cour d'Assizes, where he might testify in a case. The ornate cream and gold decor gives a Second Empire look to this café close to La Sainte Chapelle. If you're seated here, coffee is 12.50 francs, a double 25, a *café au lait* or hot chocolate 20, and capuccino 28 francs. Tea is 25 francs, a Coke 22, and sandwiches are 20 francs and up.

The **Taverne Henri IV**, a well-known wine bar in the area, would not have been neglected by Maigret. It's located at 13 Place du Pont Neuf, 75001 Paris (43.54.27.90). Métro: Pont-Neuf. The Taverne has wines available for 20 francs a glass and up. Plates of cheese, pâté, and *saucisson* are about 60 francs, including some of the excellent *pain poilâne*.

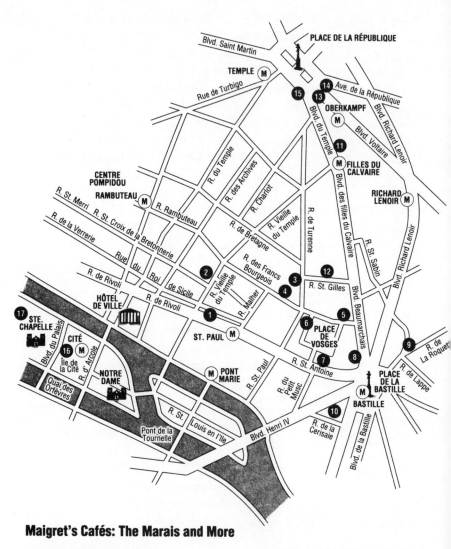

The Cafés of Paris

Maigret's Cafés: The Marais and More

1. La Tartine, 24 rue de Rivoli
2. Au Gamin de Paris, 51 rue Vieille du Temple
3. Café des Musées, 49 rue de Turenne
4. Marais Plus, 20 rue des Francs Bourgeois
5. Café Martini, 11 rue du Pas de la Mule
6. Ma Bourgogne, 19 Place des Vosges
7. L' Olivier, 6 rue Biraque
8. Flag Café, 3 bd. Beaumarchais
9. Café de L' Industrie, 16 rue St. Sabin

10. Le Temps des Cerises, 31 rue de la Cerisaie
11. Clown Bar, 114 rue Amelot
12. Caves St. Gilles, 4 rue St. Gilles
13. Le Thermomètre, 4 Place de la République
14. Le Relais d' Eguisheim, 6 Place de la République
15. La Taverne, Bar Belge, 5 Place de la République
16. Les Deux Palais, 3 bd. du Palais
17. Bar du Caveau, 17 Place Dauphine

5

The Ratman of Paris and Other Café Stories: The 1st and 6th Arrondissements

"If a person offends you, and you are in doubt as to whether it was intentional or not, do not resort to extreme measures; simply watch your chance and hit him with a brick."
—Mark Twain.

A few years ago a novel appeared on the market, entitled *The Ratman of Paris*. What most people who read it may not have realized is that there was a real "ratman" of Paris. I know there was. I saw him at least twice.

My first encounter with the Ratman happened sometime in the 1970s. I was going along the boulevard Saint-Michel with my husband. It was early summer, the birds were twittering in the trees, and all was right with the world—or so it seemed. I was soon to be shaken out of my complacency.

Suddenly, without any warning at all, an old *clochard*—we would say "vagrant" or "tramp"—in a grimy grey overcoat lurched towards me. To my horror, he was clutching a rat! As he thrust the rat at me, he seemed to be uttering loud, growling noises in a manner meant to be frightening. I don't remember exactly what I did then. I may have screamed—I almost certainly jumped into the air. From the distance came faint sounds of laughter. All of my attention was focused on one object: to get as far away from that filthy old man and his rat as soon as possible.

A couple of years later I had the chance to bring up the topic of the Ratman with a resident of Paris, a Tunisian who was doing graduate work at the Sorbonne. He, too, had seen the Ratman in action, and he was appalled: "The police should do something about him!" he insisted. Later he added: "I have seen that man with bruises on his face because some angry man has beaten him. But nothing stops him."

It wasn't for quite some time that the reason for the Ratman's little performance became evident. I was sitting at a café on the Left Bank near the spot where I myself had been caught off guard. Suddenly a commotion erupted right in front of the café. I looked up in time to see what was going on: the Ratman had selected another victim. Making his growly sounds, he suddenly thrust out the rat, and was scaring another unfortunate half to death. Several people around me laughed heartily at the sight of the unsuspecting person flailing his arms wildly in the air and jumping back, losing all dignity in the process. Somehow, viewed from a reasonable distance, the incident seemed much funnier than when I had been involved in it.

Then the motive behind the Ratman's stunt suddenly became clear: rat stowed out of sight, the old man made the rounds of the café's *terrasse*, grimy flat cap in hand. He was soliciting contributions from the same people who had been so amused by the spectacle minutes before. Several people dropped in a coin or two, still chuckling over the fellow's nerve. The Ratman was using the cafés. With their terraces crowded with people, they provided a ready-made audience for his little act.

An American friend who has lived in Paris for years was able to tell us more about the Ratman. He, too, had had his own experience. He said that he and his wife Monique had been strolling on the Left Bank when the Ratman struck:

He terrified me: I jumped and screamed when he pushed that thing in my face. Then Monique (a petite Parisienne, much shorter than her husband) looked at me and laughed. I felt ridiculous.

The man we both saw was Larry, the rat man. Originally he used to use a real dead rat. But the police made him stop doing that—so the one you saw was probably plastic. It does the same thing to people—and it certainly looks real.

The story behind "Larry's" performance has to do with *clochards*. The Parisian *clochard* is part of an old tradition of people who have made the decision to live without working. Unlike gypsies and beggars, *clochards* pride themselves on being self-supporting and not accepting handouts. Frequently they have contrived some means of raising a little money without losing their dignity. They are not criminals, and are allowed to go on in their own way, living what to some might seem an ideal life of strolling around the city with no timetables, no demanding bosses. Accepted by Parisians, they sometimes shock foreign visitors to the city who wonder who these people are, these miserable creatures: are they the rejects of society?

Not at all. In Paris it is recognized that they are people who choose to exercise their right to live without regular jobs. *Clochards* often find some way of earning a few francs. A professor who used to live near the Place Clichy reported that he would see several *clochards* who had been living in his district for about a decade. These men showed remarkable ingenuity when it came to earning money. One of them made a habit of going to sit near the entrance of a Monoprix, one of a chain of French stores, a cross between Woolworth's and Safeway. The *clochard* became known in the district. People out shopping at Monoprix would leave their bags, shopping carts, baby carriages—once even one with a baby in it! The old fellow would keep an eye on their things. "Everybody knew you could trust him," people would say. They would give their schedule: "I'll be back in 15 minutes."

"Yes, yes," the clochard would reply, continuing to drink, chat with his friends, while at the same time keeping an eye on the baby, the suitcases, or the shopping carts. Other *clochards* would make a few francs by handing in bottles to get back the deposit.

Clochards are not penniless: they all have a mandatory minimum of francs set aside, usually in a well-mended plastic pouch. This is money they never touch because the French police are able to use the "Do you have money on you?" formula for rounding up vagrants.

To avoid this sort of hassle and to lead his street life in peace, the *clochard* develops a means of making money and keeping it secure. The Ratman of Paris had achieved something: he had developed a secure means of income, perhaps seeing his performance as legitimate entertainment for cafégoers, just as sword swallowing and fire eating are accepted around the Pompidou Center as ways of making a living.

In a less spectacular or repellent way, the cafés of Paris are places of entertainment. Much of the fun is in the *bavardage* or gossip that goes on among the regulars. Once I ran into a café near the flea market at Clignancourt: I had an urgent phone call to make.

"*Est-ce qu'on peut téléphoner d'ici?*" I asked at the bar. (Can a person make a telephone call here?)

"*Oui, mais on peut boire également!*" cracked a regular. (Yes, but one can also drink). I liked that swift retort. You might say that he was establishing the priorities.

A few years ago my husband and I were sitting at a café—
or was it the *terrasse* of a restaurant?—on the Left Bank. Not
far from us were a couple—an elegant, middle-aged man flirting
with his companion, a pretty young woman in her early twenties.
They were making animated conversation and were totally
engrossed in each other. Secure with his rapid midwestern
American speech, my husband remarked more than once:

"Look at him! That guy should be ashamed. He's probably
got a wife and kids in Versailles."

I tried to hush him up, but I didn't think there was much
to worry about. Nobody had given any sign of understanding
a word of English all day. An hour or two passed, in which we
enjoyed the ambiance of this place, chatting about things we'd
seen and our plans for the next day. Finally—it was one of
those small, crowded cafés—the couple got up to go. They
had to climb past us to leave their table. Just as they were on
the point of departure, the man leaned over and said to my
husband, in perfect English: "I hope you enjoy your stay in
Paris." On his face was an ironic little smile.

An even more embarrassing café experience happened to the
late English actor and raconteur, Robert Morley. He was staying
in Paris on the Right Bank, at a hotel near the Tuileries. As he
was making a film at the time, he became quite familiar with
the area and developed the habit of patronizing a restaurant
near the elegant Place Vendôme. One evening he was on his
way to dinner, passing under the colonnades of the rue de
Rivoli. He tells the story:

As I stepped into the Arcade, I saw at a distance of two
hundred yards, a man carrying a body emerge from a lighted
doorway and, crossing the pavement, attack the colonnade
with his victim's head. Half a dozen times he swung his
human battering ram, and then casually abandoning it, let
what was left of it fall into the gutter, and returned to the
bistro.

55

Morley rushed as fast as he could to the scene to see if the victim was still breathing and to call for a doctor:

. . . . the horror and fright I felt had been replaced by righteous indignation. With scarcely a glance at the crumpled corpse, I tore into the café and into the half a dozen silent, sulky Frenchmen who sat there. A torrent of pidgin French, stage argot and half-remembered phrases from the Folies Bergère poured from my lips:

"*Bêtes sauvages! Méchants hommes! Quelle bêtise, quelle exposition formidable! . . . Appelez les gendarmes!*"

I looked around for the man who had committed the crime, but could not identify him, yet they had all been there. They had watched, they had done nothing, and now a man lay dead in the gutter, and still no one moved.

"*Ambulance!*" I shouted. "*Appelez un ambulance, vite, vite!* Very well, if you won't do it, I shall." I seized the telephone and realized I hadn't the slightest idea how to proceed. I pushed the receiver into the hands of the one I took to be the proprietor:

"*Appelez,*" I ordered. "*Appelez, vite! Pas de* nonsense! *Attendez!*"

As Morley recalled, he really had them "mesmerized":

I think in that brief instant I realized why it is Englishmen are so good in a crisis. Slow to anger, perhaps, but when we are aroused our fury is really magnificent.

"*Venez, vite!*" I reiterated, "*venez, vite!*" and, for the first time employing physical force, drove my finger deep into the patron's chest. There was a hint of menace now in the way in which he replaced the receiver on its stand. His eyes were fixed on something at the back of me. I spun round, ready for a surprise attack, to find the corpse had now got to his feet and was dusting himself off. Then he started to laugh. I can never forgive him that laugh. I like to think he was concussed, but I can never be sure. All I know is I had to pay for the telephone call before I could leave the bistro.

Where might one have seen the Ratman perform? Usually he chose cafés in the 6th arrondissement. Here are some you may enjoy:

Brasserie L'Atlas, at 11 rue de Buci, 75006 Paris (43.25.43.94). Métro: Mabillon. L'Atlas isn't glamorous, with its modern, brass-colored bar, pink and black plastic here and there, and pinball machines. What it has is a nice terrace next to a florist and opposite elegant caterers and *pâtisseries*, and reasonable prices: coffee 5 and 10 francs, tea 10 and 18, juice 14 and 20, soda and mineral water 7.50 and 20, beer 9 and 19, sandwiches 13 francs up, and hot snacks, such as *croque monsieurs*, for 22 francs. L'Atlas is very popular, and not just with tourists.

Café le Départ, 1 Place Saint-Michel, 75005 Paris (43.54.24.55). Métro: Saint-Michel. From here you can see the spire of La Sainte Chapelle.

La Chope du Marché, 7 rue Lobineau, opposite the Marché Saint-Germain. Métro: Mabillon. A pleasant bistro with a clientele that includes working-class and retired people.

L'Ecluse Grands Augustins, 15 quai des Grands Augustins, 75006 Paris (46.33.58.74). Métro: Saint-Michel. One of a chain of successful "Ecluse" cafés, worth visiting for the decor, which is exceptional.

La Palette, 43 rue de Seine, 75006 Paris (43.26.68.15). Métro: Saint-Germain-des-Prés. La Palette is a "bohemian" café, with its decor improved by the paintings displayed on the walls. Students from the Ecole des Beaux-Arts and dealers from the nearby art galleries come here. Open all day from 8 a.m. to 2 a.m. Closed in August.

La Rhumerie, 166 boulevard Saint-Germain, 75006 Paris (43.54.28.94). Founded in 1932, the Rhumerie, as its name suggests, specializes in rum. Located on the corner of the Passage de la Petite Boucherie and the boulevard Saint-Germain, the Rhumerie attempts a South Sea Islands look—and succeeds in appearing welcoming. Coffee is 12 and 13 francs, tea and hot chocolate 20, and beer 22. After 6:30 p.m. the price for coffee or tea soars to 28 francs.

Latin Odéon, opposite the métro Odéon. No provision for bar service here, but coffee is 12 and 13 francs, tea, Coke, or mineral water 20, a sandwich for 15 francs and beer for 19. Many drink prices increase drastically after 10:00 p.m.

The **Rélais Odéon** at 132 boulevard Saint-Germain, 75006 Paris (43.29.81.80). Opposite the statue of Danton and the métro Odéon and close to the famous **Procope**, this café-brasserie has kept its turn-of-the-century charm, and offers coffee for only 5.50 and 12 francs, juice and soda for 10.50 and 18.20, mineral water for 6.90 and 16.20, beer for 8.10 and 17 francs, sandwiches for 14 and 17 francs, and plats for about 50 francs.

Le Mazet, at the end of the passage—61 rue Saint-André des Arts, 75006 Paris (43.54.68.81). Métro: Odéon. This café has nice ambiance and good prices for the chic 6th arrondissement: coffee 5.50 and 10, juice 20, mineral water 20, beer 10 and 14, and a sandwich from 15 francs.

What about Robert Morley? Where might he have been headed when his humiliating adventure took place? To one of the most chic parts of the city, where some of the better choices include:

Le Castiglione, at 235 on the corner of rue Saint-Honoré and the rue de Castiglione, just off the Place Vendôme, 75001 Paris (42.60.68.22). Métro: Concorde. Light oak panelling gives Le Castiglione the look of a private club. Coffee is 6 and 13 francs, and juice just 14 and 22.

La Colombe, 2 rue de la Paix, 75002 Paris (42.61.09.69). Métro: Opéra. Next to the Place Vendôme, La Colombe is convenient and not overly priced for the area. Coffee costs 6 and 12 francs, mineral water 7.50 and 19, beer 11 and 16, a croissant 5.80 and a *pain au raisins*—the French equivalent of a Danish—7 and 8. This café has a 1950s look, with the lights mounted on cut out circles suspended from the ceiling.

La Coupe d'Or, at 330 rue Saint-Honoré, 75001 Paris (42.60.43.26). Métro: Tuileries. La Coupe is lively, popular, and open in August. Coffee is 6.50 and 12 francs, milk 22, *café au lait* 15, beer and wine 22 francs up.

Le Dauphin, 167 rue Saint-Honoré, 75001 Paris (42.60.40.11). Métro: Palais-Royal. Open noon to midnight every day except December 25 and January 1, Le Dauphin has a nineteenth-century look, with its zinc bar, cane chairs, and fan-shaped mosaic floor tiles. The Second Empire feeling is at war with the Art Deco stairs, but you can relax here anyway, given the friendly service. Coffee is 6 and 10 francs, tea 12 and 20, wine and beer 9 and 20.

Le Louis le Grand at 1 rue Louis le Grand, 75002 Paris (40.15.09.58). Métro: Opéra. Ordinary decor, but the café is airy and spacious. The low prices attract a mixed clientele, often including laborers working in the neighborhood. Coffee 5.70 and 10 francs, juice 14 and 16, mineral water 7 and 15, a sandwich 15 and 16 francs, and a lunch or *plat* 56 to 60 francs.

L'Argenterie, formerly **Le Petit Voisin**, is opposite Notre-Dame de l'Assomption at 5 rue Cambon, 75001 Paris (42.60.10.34). Métro: Concorde. Crowded with French people who like what they're getting: coffee at only 5.50 and 11 francs, and a *menu*, or full meal, at 95 francs.

Le Ver Luisant, 26 rue du Mont-Thabor, 75001 Paris (42.60.83.69). Métro: Tuileries or Concorde. A pleasant little café with a copper bar. Coffee is 5.50 and 8, a *café crème* 8 and 12, tea 12 and 15, wine 9 and 11, beer 7 and 10, and a sandwich 13 and 15 francs. Closed in August.

Lina's Sandwiches, 4 rue Cambon, 75001 Paris (40.15.94.95). Such a place might well have attracted Robert Morley, with its sun-bleached walls and sleek designer metal tables. Lina's has a superb location and reasonable prices. Coffee 6 francs, Mariage Frères tea 14, sandwiches from 18 francs. Other refreshments

The Cafés of Paris

include Coke at 8 and 10 francs, sandwiches at 18 francs and up, and delicious pastries at 15 francs.

Le Zimmer, at 1 Place du Chatelet, 75001 Paris. Go here for great views of the Tour St. Jacques, of a picturesque fountain, and, looking across the river, of Notre Dame. The people-watching is good too, from classic round brass-edged tables and comfortable wicker chairs. Coffee is 13 francs on the *terrasse*, tea 23, and beer 23. A drink at the bar here would be awkward—but who would want one, with such views?

Au Vieux Chatelet, next door at 1 Place du Chatelet 75001 Paris (42.33.79.27) offers you an even closer look at the Conciergerie and Notre Dame. Coffee 5.80 and 12 francs.

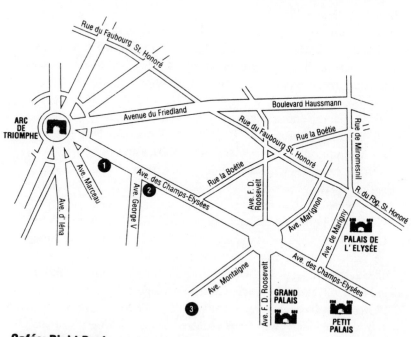

Cafés: Right Bank

1. Drugstore Champs-Elysées, 133 ave. des Champs-Elysées
2. Fouquet's, 99 ave. des Champs-Elysées
3. Bar des Théâtres, 6 ave. Montaigne

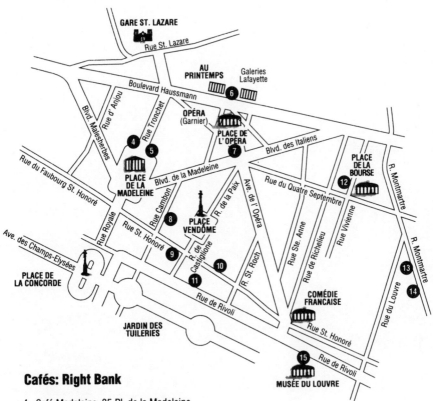

Cafés: Right Bank

4. Café Madeleine, 35 Pl. de la Madeleine
5. Fauchon, 30 Pl. de la Madeleine
6. Café Malongo, in Lafayette Monoprix, 93 rue de Provence
7. Cafe de la Paix, 12 bd. des Capucines
8. L'Argenterie; 5 rue Cambon
9. Le Castiglione, 235 rue St. Honoré
10. La Coupe d' Or, 330 rue St. Honoré
11. Angelina, 226 rue de Rivoli
12. Le Vaudeville, 29 rue Vivienne
13. Le Tambour, 41 rue Montmartre
14. Le Cochon à L' Oreille, 15 rue Montmartre
15. Le Café Marly, 93 rue de Louvre (in Louvre Museum)

61

6
From the Boulevards to Montmartre: The 9th and 18th Arrondissements

"Allais sat down at the terrace of a café on a stormy day, and said: 'Garçon, bring me a drink and turn down the wind!'"

By 1900 the fame of Montmartre, with its cafés, cabarets, and *café-concerts*, had spread to such an extent that not only Parisians, but fashionable people from all over were flocking to discover the area's nightlife for themselves. As early as 1900, guidebooks promoted Montmartre: one such book, *Guide de L'Etranger à Montmartre*, by Victor Meusy and Edmond Depas, featured many contributors who were regular patrons of the cafés. Their names read like an honor roll of the graphic arts: Willette, Steinlen, Léandre, and Grün. The Place Pigalle is at the center of Montmartre, with the boulevard de Rochechouart running along perpendicular and just behind. Important *cafés-chantants* and cabarets in Montmartre had vivid names: L'Oeil Crevé (the blinded eye), Le Moulin Rouge (the red mill), Le Ciel (heaven), located right next to L'Enfer (hell). Others known to us through posters, Le Divan Japonais, La Cigale, and Le Bruant, were nearby.

The boulevards in Paris attracted people long before Montmartre became fashionable. Lined with trees, dotted with elegant cafés, they provided the best vantage point for observing Parisian life. The boulevards once were the places to go and be seen in Paris. Bright and glamorous, with famous cafés and restaurants on either side, they extended from the Bastille to the Madeleine.

"A man will change his religion sooner than his café," observed Georges Courteline, a writer of humor at the time. Boulevard life flourished during the Second Empire, in the 1860s. The **Grand Café** and the still-popular **Café de la Paix** dominated the boulevard des Capucines, the **Café Anglais** the boulevard des Italiens. Literary men, including Alexandre Dumas, Alfred de Musset, and the Duc de Morny, gathered at a café called **Tortoni's**. One habitué of the cafés, poet Jean Moreas, described the usual routine: "You arrived at your café at 1:00 p.m. and stayed until 7:00. You went out for dinner, you came back at 9:00 and stayed until 2:00 a.m."

Desperate to keep her husband at home, one wife redecorated a room to make it look like a café, complete with small tables, rows of bottles, zinc counter, and a door marked "W.C." But it didn't satisfy her husband, who started going out again because the beer was not on tap.

On the same side of the boulevard des Italiens flourished the notorious **Maison Dorée** ("Gilded House") and the **Café Riche**. They were both high-priced; the Maison Dorée was owned by a man named Hardy. This gave rise to the comment that one must be "very rich to dine at the Hardy, and very hardy to dine at the Riche."

Actress and author Cornelia Otis Skinner observed that there was a particular sort of humor associated with the *boulevardier*, or frequenter of the boulevards. She described the *boulevardier* as:

> Parisien, his wit was Parisien, his outlook was bounded by the Boulevard itself . . . its cafés, its theatres, its easy access to the rest of the city, but no further than the Bois. He was the man of bright sophistication, the man sharply aware of the present scene.

When someone back in Paris after a trip to Italy started raving about Venice and its canals, *boulevardier* Tristan Bernard was heard to say: "Paris wouldn't be too bad either, if only the Municipal Council would open up the sewers."

One evening at Maxim's, Georges Feydeau, a wit and a writer of farces, was heard complaining that he had been served a lobster with only one claw. Upon protesting to the waiter, he was told that lobsters are combative and sometimes fight each other in the tank. "Ah?" responded Feydeau. "Then take this one away and bring me the winner!"

Created by Baron Haussman in the 1860s, the boulevards began to be seen as the place from which to see Paris at its best. In a letter written in July of 1876, Henry James spoke about "the broom of Monsieur Haussmann," which had swept through the city, "widening and straightening the streets." As late as the 1930s the Baedeker guide to Paris recommended the Grands Boulevards as a place for visitors to spend their late afternoons and evenings. For Henry James, the boulevard cafés were what made Paris endurable in the summer:

> Of all great cities, Paris is the most tolerable in hot weather . . . there are a hundred persuasions to keeping out of doors. You are not obliged to sit on a "stoop" or curbstone, as in New York. The boulevards are a long chain of cafés, each one with its little promontory of chairs and tables projecting into the sea of asphalt . . . . There you may dine in the Champs

Elysées at a table set under the trees, beside an ivied wall, and almost believe you are in the country.

Alfred de Musset described the boulevard de Ghent in 1840:

This dirty, dusty strip of street is one of the rare points on the surface of the globe where pleasure of every kind can be had for the asking . . . restaurants, cafés, theaters, public baths, gambling dens—all are within a yard or two . . . The boulevard de Ghent doesn't come alive before noon. The dandies arrive soon after twelve, and they come into the Café Tortoni by the back door to avoid the stock market people who crowd in at the front . . . . They make a lot of noise, and when they leave, it is with an impenetrable air and in freshly varnished boots.

At five o'clock, the boulevard changes its character and empties completely . . . . Rented carriages unload their cargo of English families at the Café de Paris, which they believe to be still all the rage . . . . At 8:30, tumult: a hundred digestions work overtime, a hundred cigars glow in the dark, there is a squeal of two hundred boots, hats are not quite on straight . . . waistcoat buttons burst . . . . At 11:30 the theaters are over and people trample one another under foot to get an ice cream at Tortoni's before going to bed. At midnight a strayed dandy—worn out by his day—sinks into his chair, crosses his long legs, drinks a glass of lemonade between yawns, pats a shoulder here and there . . . and leaves. The lights go out. A last cigarette by moonlight, and everyone leaves for home.

"There is nothing so bad or so good that you will not find
Englishmen doing it; but you will never find an Englishman in
the wrong. He does everything on principle."
—George Bernard Shaw

A hundred years ago the big spenders on the boulevards of
Paris were English. Along the rue de Rivoli, great hotels catered
to their appetites with English breakfasts and afternoon teas.
Later in the day, English ladies patronized the great houses of
fashion, Worth and LaFerrière. They might later go on to lunch
at Le Grand Véfour near the Palais Royal. After shopping or
sightseeing, most would wind up at the cafés on the rue Scribe
or the rue de la Paix.

Writing on April 22, 1876, Henry James was not enthusiastic
about the onslaught of Englishmen into Paris: "Early on Monday
the British tourist made his appearance on the boulevards, and
he has been visible at every turn ever since. He has fairly taken
possession of the city, and if his presence is fleeting it is, so to
speak, intense."

The boulevards remained interesting for people who wanted
to explore Paris on foot. Yet the cafés there became like private
clubs, reserved for the upper classes. Georges Montorgueil had
written: "It was an audacious fellow or a boor who dared set
foot in the old Café de Paris without a sponsor. Tortoni's had
its own set, and no one felt at home at the Grand Balcon until
after the proper introductions had been made." The crowd that
assembled at the Café Anglais after the theater was aristocratic,
consisting of such regulars as Prince Galitzine and the Marquis
d'Orange.

Late in the century, when the boulevards began to attract
the upper middle class, they were abandoned by the aristocracy.
Tortoni's, "the most dandified café in Paris," according to Henry
James, went out of business in 1893. The Café de Paris closed
in 1896, and the Café de Madrid in the following year. Café
society would never be the same again.

Look through the windows of **Le Grand Véfour**—there you can still glimpse the elegance of the great cafés at 17 rue de Beaujolais, 75001 Paris (42.96.56.27). A café in the 1760s, Le Grand Véfour welcomed a clientele as distinguished as Napoleon and Josephine. Now it is an elegant and expensive restaurant.

If you are on or near the Grands Boulevards, where do you go nowadays for coffee or a snack? Unfortunately, the Grands Boulevards have been taken over so completely by cars and the resulting pollution that a leisurely afternoon sipping coffee on the *terrasse* of a café there might seem out of the question. Still, you could try:

Cafe de la Paix, 12 boulevard des Capucines, 70009 Paris (42.68.12.13). Métro: Opéra. Near American Express. This famous and historic café was designed by Charles Garnier, the same architect responsible for the famous Opéra across the street. A small espresso here costs 26 francs. Still, the café is worth seeing for its elegant Second Empire interior. It's also convenient to the Roissybus, a quick and easy way to get to and from Charles de Gaulle airport. You may want to make it your first or last stop in Paris.

L'Entr'acte, 1 rue Auber, 75009 Paris (47.42.26.25). Métro: Opéra. Reasonable prices, friendly service, and, from the first floor, a stunning view of the old Opéra make L'Entr'acte a good choice for this area. Coffee 5.80 and 13 francs.

Bar des Théâtres, 6 avenue Montaigne, 75008 Paris (47.23.34.63). Métro: Alma-Marceau. Although not on a boulevard, the Bar des Théâtres has something of the ambiance of a classic "boulevard" café. Facing the Théâtre des Champs-Elysées, the Bar des Théâtres welcomes a good number of actors among its regular clientele, which has been also known to include top models and some of the greatest names in the world of *haute couture*—Chanel, Givenchy, Ungaro, and Dior. The Bar des Théâtres has a classic zinc bar and reasonable prices.

Espace Café Bleu, 15 Place du Faubourg Saint-Honoré, 75008

Paris (44.71.32.32). Métro: Madeleine. Right across the street from the legendary saddle and silk scarf maker, Hermès, Espace Café Bleu is on the lower level of Lanvin. Sink back in the comfortable armchairs in an air-conditioned interior featuring a postmodern, Art Deco-inspired look, in heavy cream, deep blue and blond oak. At the end of a warm summer afternoon of shopping or just looking, this café underground is just the thing. Espresso is 18 francs, tea, Coke, and mineral water 20, and beer 25.

Fauchon, 30 Place de la Madeleine, 75008 Paris (47.42.60.11). Métro: Madeleine. With its good location near the old Opéra, a stop at Fauchon for coffee—and the small chocolate thrown in—will invigorate you for further exploration of the boulevards. A more detailed description is in the chapter "A Cheapskate's Guide."

The **Café Madeleine**, at 35 Place de la Madeleine, 75008 Paris (42.65.21.91), is a pleasant alternative to Fauchon's with coffee for 6 and 13 francs, and a view onto the Place de la Madeleine.

Le Paris London, 16 Place de la Madeleine, 75008 Paris (47.42.33.92). Métro: Madeleine. Le Paris London is a simple little café-bar-brasserie beside Fauchon. The coffee must be good, because I saw the cooks from Fauchon taking their afternoon coffee break here. Open from 7 a.m. to 7 p.m., the Paris London recalls the 1950s, with its zinc and oak bar, globe lights, mirrors and shiny surfaces. Coffee is 5.20 and 11 francs, beer 11 and 21, fruit juice and mineral water 15 and 21. Sandwiches are 14 francs, and a variety of other light lunches—a *croque monsieur*, a club sandwich—cost 35 francs. It's a friendly place.

Changing Money - the Bourse

As mentioned in the Introduction, a good place for changing your traveller's cheques is at the moneychangers on the rue Vivienne, which runs in front of the Bourse. Check out:

Gallopin, 40 rue Notre-Dame-des-Victoires, just behind the Bourse, or stock exchange. Since its regulars are men who work at the Bourse or at nearby *change* offices, the place has something of a "private club" ambiance.

La Cave Drouot, 8 rue Drouot, 75002 Paris (47.70.83.38). Métro: Richelieu-Drouot. On the corner of the rue Rossini, the Cave Drouot is conveniently near the Bourse. Stop by for a cup of coffee or a glass of wine, and a plate of the famous *poilâne* bread with a few slices of ham. Friendly service. Open from 7:30 a.m. to 9 p.m., the Cave is closed on Sundays.

Also near the Bourse, close enough to Agence France Presse to be interesting to its journalists, are:

Le Vaudeville, at 29 rue Vivienne, 75002 Paris (40.20.04.62). Métro: Bourse. Don't be put off by the tablecloths—in the afternoon, this becomes a real café. A brass bar with green marble, faux walnut square tables, comfortable chairs, and outstanding service: "Make yourselves at home," said the waiter as he ushered us to a table. Coffee is 5.50 and 8 francs, beer 9.50 and 13. Reasonable prices for a very special place.

L'Aiglon, 12 rue Vivienne, 75002 Paris (42.60.08.83). Métro: Bourse. A small, intimate café-bar, open from 7 a.m. to 7 p.m., closed on weekends and the last 2 weeks in August. Coffee is 5 and 7 francs, beer 9 and 12.

At the nearby **Riva Sandwich**, 2 rue Colonnes, 75002 Paris (42.60.40.81), sandwiches are from 22 francs apiece. This is a good place for a quick lunch in a clean green and white setting if you're on the run and still in the area of the Bourse.

Back in the Shopping District:

Ladurée, 16 rue Royale, 75008 Paris (42.60.21.79). Métro: Madeleine. While not exactly inexpensive, Ladurée has charm, charm and more charm! It's worth a visit just to contemplate the classic panelled and mirrored interior. Sample the outstanding pastries while sipping a coffee—in this place, the experience is well worth the 18-franc cost.

Le Grain de Café, 4 Place de l'Opéra, 75009 Paris (42.66. 99.78). Métro: Opéra. Here is a source for a variety of excellent coffees at about 6 francs a cup, in the expensive Opéra area. Good pastries and sandwiches are available. Open at 6 a.m. and closed Sundays.

Le Salon du Chocolat, 11 boulevard de Courcelles, 75008 Paris (45.22.07.27). This may be the answer for all of us chocoholics out there. A hot drink and pastry will cost around 50 francs.

When *cafés-concerts* and cabarets became all the rage, it was to Montmartre that the English tourists flocked. Even the Prince of Wales attended the **Moulin Rouge** and watched the antics of La Goulue, and it is said that she flung one of her coarse jests at him.

In the 1880s and 1890s, as later, people were attracted to Paris because they sensed that it was one of the freest cities anywhere. This feeling became a sirens' song for creative people from all over the world. Right then, at the end of the nineteenth century, it was this perception which made Montmartre a world capital for pleasure seekers.

Why Montmartre? What was there about this area to make it a center for entertainment in the 1890s and beyond? For artists it had become attractive ever since the founding of La Ruche (the beehive), a housing venture with tiny, cell-like rooms. Artists could have a place to stay at minimal cost while they created their works in the clean air and country setting. But several other factors contributed to the development of Montmartre as a place associated with abandon, escape, and decadent pleasure-seeking. Not the least of these was the establishment of what was to become a celebrated cabaret.

On October 6, 1889, the **Moulin Rouge** opened for the first time and made the can-can famous. Although invented years before, the can-can was revived. It seemed to symbolize the spirit of Paris at the time, with all of its daring to disobey rules and flout conventions.

The can-can or *chahut*, as Parisians called it, was first seen at the **Moulin de la Galette**, a rough, working-class establishment patronized by pimps and thieves. (The Moulin de la Galette still survives as an Italian restaurant, between the rue Lepic and the avenue Junot, right beside the Maison Tristan Tzara). But the can-can really developed at another dance hall, the **Elysée-Montmartre**, at 72 boulevard de Rochechouart, where the band leader had the bright idea of combining the *chahut* with a Second Empire quadrille.

Raymond Rudorff, in *Belle Epoque*, described the new dance:

> As the band struck up the girls would come out to the center of the dance floor, start with a few relatively simple steps, and then work up to a frenzy, spinning around like tops, turning cartwheels sometimes, and punctuating their gyrations with the famous high kick, the *"port d'armes"* [shoulder arms] when the dancer would stand on the toes of one foot, holding the other foot as high as possible with one hand. It was a noisy, stamping dance, it was earthy and animal, performed to a rough and ready clientele in an atmosphere of tobacco smoke, sweat, and cheap perfume . . .

The can-can attained the zenith of its popularity under La Goulue, a dancer immortalized in the paintings of Toulouse-Lautrec. La Goulue—actually Louise Weber—was a coarse, boisterous dancer from the working class. Georges Montorgueil observed her at the time and described her as "pink and blonde, about 18 years of age, with a wilful, vicious and ruddy-hued baby face . . . a mouth gluttonous and sensual, a look shameless and provoking . . . such was the little washerwoman who had rediscovered the can-can as though by instinct."

When La Goulue danced the can-can, she made it look erotic and naughty. According to Montorgueil, attention was riveted on her because of the "display of bare flesh" and "the turbulent swirl of her underclothes as she purposefully allows a glimpse of a large sample of her naked skin between garter and the first fold of her petticoat . . . . The invitation is brutal, blunt, without feminine grace, almost bestial, in this fleshy girl as she outlines the lascivious meanderings of her sullied imagination with a twist of her limbs . . ."

Other observers described La Goulue as a "foulmouthed guttersnipe," but observed that when she danced, she was transfigured. As Henri Perruchot noted in his biography of Toulouse-Lautrec, she kicked towards the ceiling and "her petticoats boiled like foam; she was a bacchante, possessed by rhythm, whirling disdainfully, indifferently, among a circle of infatuated men."

For Mark Twain in *Innocents Abroad*, the can-can was one of the sights of Paris, something not to be missed. Twain tried hard not to appear awed by anything he saw in Europe. He related his impressions:

The dance had begun, and we adjourned to the temple. Within it was a drinking saloon, and all around it was a broad, circular platform for the dancers. I backed up against the wall of the temple and waited. Twenty sets formed, the music struck up, and then—I placed my hands before my face for very shame. But I looked through my fingers. They were dancing the renowned "Cancan." A handsome girl in the set before me tripped forward lightly to meet the opposite gentleman, tripped back again, grasped her dresses vigorously on both sides with her hands, raised them pretty high, danced an extraordinary jig that had more activity and exposure about it than any jig I ever saw before, and then, drawing her clothes still higher, she advanced gaily to the center and launched a vicious kick full at her vis-a-vis that must infallibly have removed his nose if he had been seven feet high. It was a mercy he was only six. The idea of it is to dance as wildly, as noisily, as furiously as you can; to expose yourself as much as possible if you are a woman; and kick as high as you can, no matter which sex you belong to.

Some of the regulars in Montmartre cafés were infamous, not so much for how they danced as for their practical jokes. The story is told of a ball that was coming up at the **Chat Noir**. Jean Lorrain, a young man from the country, very concerned about looking correct and fitting in with Parisians, sought out his friend Alphonse Allais, the main organizer of the event:

> "Tell me, Alphy, what should I come in, a regular suit or in drag? The invitation doesn't say anything about it."
> "In drag, in drag," Allais responded. "It'll be a requirement."

Later that evening, well-dressed men in suits and pretty girls in blouses and skirts observed a strange creature who entered, clad in a bathing suit of silk and wearing a wreath of flowers on his head and a belt of grape leaves at his hips. Faithful to the directions given him by Allais, it was Jean Lorrain.

A wild burst of laughter greeted him.

The cabarets, famous or infamous, are gone; tourists swarm about the Place du Tertre, where they buy paintings that could have been turned out in a factory. Yet there are still some places worth seeking out in Montmartre:

La Crêpe à Pic, 35 rue Lepic, 75018 Paris (42.55.95.95). Métro: Blanche. A small but appealing *salon de thé* and restaurant specializing in crêpes from 14 francs up. Here coffee is only 9 francs, milk and tea 12, hot chocolate and Coke 15, and half a carafe of table wine, 20 francs. La Crêpe is open from 12 to 3 and from 5 to 11 p.m.

Da Graziano, at 85 rue Lepic, 75018 Paris (46.06.84.77). Da Graziano is a restaurant located in the Moulin de la Galette, one of the last two moulins or mills surviving in Montmartre. Appealing because of its historic interest, Da Graziano also provides 150 and 189-franc menus. Open daily.

Aux Négociants, 27 rue Lambert, 75018 Paris (46.06.15.11). It would be worth moving to Montmartre just to be close to this authentic neighborhood bistrot and Au Relais below. There's a real feeling of hospitality here. A lunchtime plat, about 60 francs, cheese plates 30 francs. On the walls are framed black-and-white photos by the famous photographer, Robert Doisneau, who was a friend of the genial proprietor. Coffee 5.50 and 9 francs.

Au Relais—Le Bistrot d'Edouard, 48 rue Lamarck 75018 Paris (46.06.68.32) is another oustanding bistrot with good food at reasonable prices. Lunches are available for 65 francs, coffee is 6 and 10 francs. The proprietors like to chat; on my last visit, Madame entertained me with a description of their summer trip to the U.S.

Le Carrousel, 8 rue des Trois Frères, 75018 Paris (42.23.82.62). Pleasant bakery with *salon de thé.* Coffee 9 francs.

Le Nord-Sud, opposite the métro Jules Joffrin in Montmartre and next to the town hall, offers coffee at 5.90 and 11, decaf at 12, hot chocolate at 22 francs, and beer for 8 and 18 francs. A shiny, modern café offering reasonably priced lunches.

La Maison Rose, 2 rue de l'Abreuvoir, 75018 Paris (42.57.66.75). Métro: Lamarck-Caulaincourt. This is the house that was once Utrillo's *atelier*—check it out for lunch.

Le Maquis, 69 rue Caulaincourt, 75018 Paris (42.59.76.07). Métro: Lamarck-Caulaincourt. Orders taken until 10 p.m. Closed Sunday and Monday. Lunch is available for about 50 francs. Desserts are made on the premises.

A la Mère Catherine, 6 Place du Tertre, 75018 Paris (46.06.32.69). Go to métro Abbesses and take the funicular up to Sacré Coeur. To get to the Mère Catherine you have to cut through the crowds of tourists in the Place. The food is average—but you don't go to Montmartre for great cuisine. With its deep rose façade and red-and-white gingham table-cloths, the Mère Catherine is attractive, and its prices are not out of line for the Place du Tertre. Coffee is 16 and 18 francs, hot chocolate 18, tea 16, beer 22 and 25 francs, soda and wine 20 francs.

Also on the Place du Tertre:

La Bohème du Tertre, with coffee at 20 and 24 francs, soda 19, juice 20, beer 18, and wine 20 francs and up.

Au Clairon des Chasseurs, 3 Place du Tertre, 75018 Paris (42.62.40.08), where coffee starts at just 12 francs, a "double" 22, beer 18, wine 22, and sandwiches are from 18 francs up.

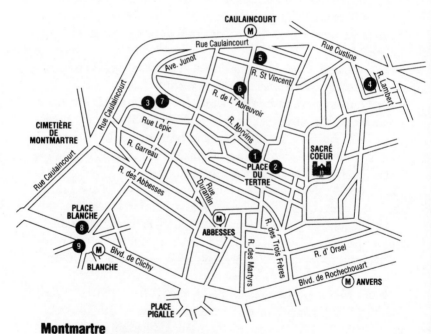

Montmartre

1. Chez la Mère Catherine, 6 Place du Tertre
2. Au Clairon des Chasseurs, 3 Place du Tertre
3. Da Graziano, 85 rue Lepic
4. Aux Négociants, 27 rue Lambert
5. Le Lapin Agile, 22 rue des Saules
6. La Maison Rose, 2 rue de L' Abreuvoir
7. La Crêpe à Pic, 35 rue Lepic
8. Le Moulin Rouge, 82 bd. de Clichy
9. Batifol, 3 Place Blanche

7

A Place Unfit for Ladies

"The best cafés may be with propriety visited by ladies, though Parisiennes of the upper class rarely patronize them. Some of those on the north side of the Boulevard Montparnasse should, however, be avoided, as the society there is far from select."
—Baedeker, 1904

So went the general impression of many cafés in Paris at the turn of the century. Even in the twenties, the double standard continued in full force. Sisley Huddleston, an English newspaperman who was the chief correspondent for the *Times* of London and well acquainted with Paris described:

> . . . a hard-faced American girl not more than twenty years of age. She was well educated, shrewd, alive to all modern movements. She was travelling alone, and happened to be staying in the same hotel as [Sherwood] Anderson. In my studio she sat rigid, her mask-like face never changing its expression. She placidly smoked her cigarette in a long tube and sipped her brandy.

Huddleston reported the girl's behavior to Sherwood Anderson and the writer was not surprised:

> Yes, they are like that . . . . The younger folk seem to feel nothing. Now if you or I, sitting by a girl in our youth, had placed an arm around her waist, she would either have responded coyly or have smacked our face. I believe today that the same girl would not even be aware . . . . She would go on smoking her cigarette and sipping her brandy.

In his book *Paris Salons, Cafés, Studios*, Huddleston expressed his sense of shock at the women of the 1920s and their attitudes, represented by that one young woman he met in 1928. He complained:

> But . . . in external appearance there is no longer any difference between the honest woman—and the other kind of woman. They have both the same kind of dress and the same kind of manners—unless perhaps one should say that the other kind are generally better-behaved and more discreet. In all these public places you meet women, old and young, whose appearance is blatantly intended to be attractive to men . . . . Bare arms, bare necks, legs uncovered to the knee or beyond, are so conspicuous a feature of the theatre, the restaurant, the salon, that they almost pass unnoticed.

He quoted his friend Paul Gaultier, director of the variety show the Revue Bleue, as equally shocked by the scandalous changes in society:

> Indeed in our day *les femmes galantes* [call girls] set the mode—which the rest surpass. The courtesan, however successful, used to be despised. Today she is envied, admired, invited, flattered. *Bourgeoises* and *grandes dames* imitate her. That is their principal preoccupation. Virtuous *mères de famille* try

to resemble her . . . . The fault does not altogether lie with the feminine sex. Husbands expect their wives to possess the sophisticated charm, in toilette, appearance, speech, gestures, of—the French word must here be used—*poules* [prostitutes]. Modesty has disappeared.

The sixteenth-century forerunners of the fin-de-siècle cafés were the wineshops, where ladies were not supposed to go. These shops were run by merchants of wine, beer, and lemonade. Gradually wineshops stopped attracting the middle class. A contemporary observer pointed out that they were frequented mostly by soldiers, workers, coachmen, lackeys, and prostitutes.

The *commissaire* of the Halles district noted in 1752 only eighteen women who went alone to wineshops. Four sold fruit or fish locally, two worked in the local fishmarket, one was married to the water carrier, and four more were "seamstresses." Probably at least one of these was a prostitute. The rest were merchants' wives. A popular expression of the time was *"elle courait les cafés"* (she ran around cafés). This was another way of saying that the person being described was a woman of low morals.

Julian Street's *Where Paris Dines*, published in 1929, devoted a chapter to "Gay Restaurants: restaurants with dancing, entertainment, or both." In his list of restaurants said to be "gay" or lively—was the **Café des Ambassadeurs**, 1 avenue Gabriel, Carré des Champs Elysées, which he considered brilliant but outrageously expensive. The **Café de Paris**, at 41 avenue de L'Opéra, was one of the best and most high-priced places to eat. Although **Maxim's**, at 3 rue Royale, could not really be called a café, it rated special mention: Street noted that it had been known for years as a symbol of "nocturnal dissipation," even if it dated from only 1893. The original proprietor had originated the plan "of encouraging the presence of a class of women, more or less attached to the establishment, whose business it was to attract male customers."

Some of the most influential women in Paris in the 1920s

were lesbians, who would not have been considered "ladies" at the time. Certain cafés in the Montparnasse area became known as hangouts for lesbians. One was the Sélect, where in 1936 Simone de Beauvoir mentioned that she and Sartre would go and sit "among the crop-haired Lesbians, who wore ties and even monocles on occasion; but such exhibitionism struck us as affected."

Canadian writer Morley Callaghan recalled in his reminiscences of the summer of 1929 that Pauline Hemingway, Ernest's second wife, disliked the atmosphere of the cafés and had suggested to Morley and Loretto Callaghan that sitting at cafés was not the proper thing to do. He commented: "For our part we were not concerned with the impression we might be making, nor with the fact that French ladies of quality did not sit at the cafés." The Callaghans had discovered that at cafés like the Coupole, the Lilas, and the Sélect, they could get good food, enjoy good company, and observe the eternal carnival that was Paris in 1929.

> *"Here, fatty, place your fat carcass next to Madame. And you, you long sausage, put your skeleton between these fools who're laughing like a couple of idiots at God knows what!"*
> —Aristide Bruant

This was the sort of compliment a lady might expect in the **Café Mirleton** in the 1880s. After Aristide Bruant bought the Mirleton in 1885, he found that a flood of insulting remarks, coarse comments, and vulgar jokes did not repel customers, but rather enticed them to come in and stay. A friendly observer, writer Francis Carco, has left us a detailed description of Bruant, saying that he

> . . . sings as he walks or walks as he sings. The clients join in the chorus. When customers come into the café, we shout abuse at them and they are happy. Last night these very

80

same spectators were: "My Lords, my Gentlemen, your Highnesses" and they were happy. Tonight they are at Bruant's who calls them by names of fish, waders or ruminants, according to their sex, and they are and still are happy.

For a lady in the 1880s, a barrage of insults might not be the worst: she could find herself sitting next to a streetwalker. When the police were rounding up prostitutes in Montmartre, Aristide Bruant was sympathetic to the plight of these women. He would often find room for them in his cabaret, scattering them among his regular customers so that they would pass unnoticed. Bruant made these outcasts the subjects of his songs:

> There they are
> Who have lost their charms,
> And who have
> Not a penny in their stockings . . . .
> Streetwalkers,
> Pavement pacers,
> They walk in the night
>
> When it is dark
> On the sidewalk
> On the sidewalk.
>
> They have no more bread
> And no more fuel
> They pray to the Lord
> Who is a good lad
> To warm up their beds.

Aristide Bruant was described by Edmond Goncourt, who saw him at a party in 1892 and was scandalized:

He appeared wearing a blood red silk shirt, with a velvet jacket and long polished leather gaiters. Beneath a center parting, fine, regular features, dark, velvety eyes in the shadows of deep brows, a short, straight nose, a dark, matt complexion . . . .

What he sang before the society women who were there was quite indescribable. This ignoble lyricism consisted of foul adjectives, dirty words, purulent slang, the vocabulary of sordid brothels and clinics for venereal diseases. You had to see Bruant belching this out in his brassy voice, see him as I saw him, in profile, the look in the sinister shadow of his perfidiously gentle eye, the coal black nostril of the tiptilted nose, and the movements of the facial muscles, reminiscent of the jaw movements of a wild beast eating carrion.

Meanwhile I, for all that I am no prude, had the impression that I was attending a prison concert . . . and to think that those society women, without the protection of a fan, without even a blush on their cheeks, listening to the man from close to, smiled and clapped their pretty aristocratic hands at words no different from the obscene scribblings on walls from which they avert their eyes.

Bruant has remained famous for the song he wrote about yet another Montmartre *café-concert*, Le Chat Noir: "*Je cherche fortune autour du Chat noir*" (I'm seeking my fortune near the Black Cat), as well as for the arresting posters by Toulouse-Lautrec.

Now that Toulouse-Lautrec's work is famous, it may be surprising to think that Aristide Bruant helped to promote his friend's career. In 1892, Bruant had asked Lautrec to create a poster to advertise his forthcoming appearance at **Les Ambassadeurs**. When Lautrec had created his best known poster of Bruant, in a swirling black cape with red scarf and signature broad brimmed black hat, the owner of the café was reluctant to use it for publicity. Bruant had to threaten not to appear unless his friend's poster was used. Lautrec's masterpiece was displayed all over Paris, and he was on his way to being considered one of the greatest artists of the poster.

In another unforgettable poster, the singer stands in his characteristic black with his back to the onlookers. Here Bruant is identified forever with a café owned by another man, Rudolphe Salis. Salis had popularized the idea of Montmartre as a center of entertainment. It was a magnet for young Toulouse-Lautrec, who patronized the **Elysée**, the **Chat Noir**, and the **Mirleton**, using them as sources for his paintings. Finally, an exasperated relative, an uncle, expressed his consternation over what was happening to the noble Toulouse-Lautrec name: "For the honor of the name," he said, "it would be better if he selected his models elsewhere than in Montmartre."

By 1910 a group of artists including Picasso had left Montmartre and were meeting at the café **Ermitage** on the boulevard Rochechouart. Georges Bernier mentions in his book on artists' cafés that in the same café was a long table, "occupied by some extremely alarming pimps, keeping watch on the comings and goings of their girls on the boulevard." Usually the two groups, the pimps and the artists, stayed separate and avoided quarrels— but not always. It is reported that Picasso got respect when one day he felled someone who had jostled him with a single punch.

A.J. Liebling, the celebrated journalist, had a great appetite for all of the pleasures of Paris. He described in *Between Meals* what might happen to the "girls"—Liebling's word—who frequented the cafés in the late 1920s. He compared them to country artisans: "They took money for their services, but only when they felt like working. On occasion they would accept payment in kind—a dinner or a pair of stockings—but then, as often as not, they would ask you to lend them their current week's room rent."

The worst situation possible would be if one of them attracted the attention of the *police des moeurs* [vice squad]. As Liebling told it:

Once the cops of this unsavory group picked up a girl without visible means of support they would force her to register. They they would give her a card that subjected her to a set of rules.

"Once a girl has the card she is bound to infract the rules," the girls said. "We are all so lazy. She misses a couple of visits; she is subject to heavy penalties. Then comes blackmail. The police put her to work for chaps who give them a cut. Hop, then, no more chattering with student friends who have no money.

"It's the pavement for her, and turn over the receipts to the mackerel at five o'clock in the morning. The police have opened another account."

Liebling commented that he was glad to know how things were, since it helped him "to understand the cops, who run true to form everywhere."

Some of the famous cafés of Montmartre, now no longer cafés, were:

Le Chat Noir, at 82 boulevard de Rochechouart. Métro: Anvers.

L'Elysée-Montmartre, at 72 boulevard de Rochechouart.

So, are there still cafés that women should avoid in the 1990s? Every woman will have her own list of least appreciated places, whether it's a matter of dreary interiors, brusque service, or excessively high prices.

The rue Saint-Denis is the current red-light district of Paris, particularly the part of it which runs from the Porte Saint-Denis to the corner of the rue de Turbigo and the rue Etienne. A street of luxury boutiques in the nineteenth century, Saint-Denis never quite recovered from the creating of the boulevard de Sébastopol by Haussmann. A garment district by day, the area is best avoided by night.

84

A café in the area:

Le Dauphin Bleu, 75002 Paris (42.21.98.40). Situated at the corner of the rue St-Denis and rue Etienne-Marcel, Le Dauphin is frequented by retired people who live in the district and also by a certain number of streetwalkers who go there between assignations.

Not in the area, but on our list:

Fouquet's, at 99 avenue des Champs-Elysées, 75008 Paris (47.23.70.60). Métro: Georges-V. Some may consider Fouquet's worth visiting, despite its high prices—coffee is 25 francs—for the superb view of the Arc de Triomphe and of the Champs-Elysées generally. Women may wish to boycott it regardless: the sign *"Les femmes seules ne sont pas admises au bar"*—single women will not be served at the bar—is posted. Supposedly a policy to protect women, this only succeeds in insulting them. Let us take our business elsewhere.

Pigalle was the traditional red-light district in Paris. If you are in the area—some friends got booked into a hotel there when they were staying in Paris with their two children—you will see a real "slice of life" at:

Le Sans-Souci, 65 rue Pigalle, 75009 Paris (48.74.37.28). Métro: Pigalle. A varied clientele: *"bourgeois"* and people of the street rub elbows here.

Tabac des Deux Moulins, 15 rue Lepic, 75018 Paris (42.54.90.50). Métro: Blanche. The Tabac was described in Paris's *Free Voice* magazine as being "between the tourist hordes of Sacre Coeur and the frantic sleaze of Pigalle," a place where "all types . . . and you find them all here . . . drop in for a quiet, quick drink before doing whatever has to be done that night."

But reasonable alternatives exist:

Dogs, at 7 rue Cossonnerie, 75001 Paris (42.21.37.24). Métro: Châtelet-Les Halles. On the corner of the rue de la Cossonnerie and the rue Saint-Denis, Dogs tries for a 1950s look, in light green, black, and cream. As you might expect, the speciality is hot dogs—if you want a drink, Coke is 14 to 26 francs, mineral water 10 to 20, beer 18 and 24, a milk shake 26 and 36, and hot chocolate or tea, 14 francs.

Front Page, 58 rue Saint-Denis, 75001 Paris (42.36.98.69). Métro: Châtelet-Les Halles. The Front Page is a decent possibility if you find yourself on the rue Saint-Denis. Wildly popular, the Front Page has red-and-white-checked tablecloths, a dark interior but a large *terrasse* set off by potted trees. Coffee is 10 francs, water 14, juice 16, tea 20, and beer 25.

And, following in the great tradition of Aristide Bruant and the *café-chantant*, **Scop Merle Moqueur** rated special mention by poet Dominique Joubert, interviewed in *Le Quotidien de Paris*. Like the Chat Noir, the Merle Moqueur has had its own newsletter, with articles about poetry and songs. Here you can hear the songs of Frenchmen Brassens and Vincent Absil, with possibly a little Bob Dylan thrown in. The Merle Moqueur is at 11 rue Butte aux Cailles, 75013 Paris (45.65.12.43). Métro: Corvisart.

8

Artists' Cafés: Montmartre and Montparnasse

"A picture is a poem without words."—Horace

D id cafés encourage the development of art, or did the new movement in art support the rise in cafés? Certainly, some cafés in Paris became known because the artists who went there drew on them as subjects for their work. These cafés were pictured in paintings that are now familiar to us all. Who can think of the **Moulin Rouge**, the **Chat Noir**, or the **Café des Ambassadeurs** without recalling a great artist? A flowering of art depicted cafés in the 1870s and 1880s. Renoir's *Moulin de la Galette* showed the dance hall in Montmartre in 1876. In 1877, Degas produced *The Café-Concert at the Ambassadeurs*, and Manet's *Bar at the Folies Bergères* appeared in 1882. But it was Toulouse-Lautrec whose series of paintings and posters of Jane Avril, Yvette Guilbert, and La Goulue dancing put Montmartre on the map. Lautrec spent much of his time there, frequenting the **Elysée**, the **Chat Noir**, and the **Mirleton**. Later at the **Moulin Rouge** the dancing of La Goulue and Jane Avril captivated him, and inspired some of his greatest works.

Even before the Belle Epoque and the excitement centering on Montmartre, Manet had started to frequent the **Café de Bade**, beginning around 1861. It was his headquarters for years. Eventually a group of painters moved to the quieter **Café Guerbois**, but not before Dante Gabriel Rossetti had stopped in at the Café de Bade on a trip from England and been thoroughly shocked by what he considered the decadence of French art.

Several influential artists lived near or in Montmartre. In the mid-1860s, Manet resided on the boulevard des Batignolles. Ten years later, he moved to the rue de Saint-Petersbourg and afterwards to the rue d'Amsterdam. Degas lived on the rues Blanche and Frochot, and Renoir had a studio at 35 rue Saint-Georges. Picasso first lived on the rue Gabrielle, with several of his friends from Spain staying at the Moulin de la Galette.

The painters who became known as the Impressionists began to join forces through regular meetings in cafés. This came to pass before they started to give exhibitions together in the 1870s. Their cafés were the **Guerbois** and the **Nouvelle Athènes**. The Guerbois, at 9 grande rue des Batignolles, was near the Place de Clichy. A contemporary observer noted that the dozen or so artists who gathered there included Degas, Renoir, Monet, and Pissarro.

Of Manet, Henry Shelley wrote: "His pictures had so violated the aesthetic canons of the day that when he was seen on the streets people turned round to gaze at him, and his advent at a fashionable café created a general murmur of uncomplimentary comment." He was regarded by public and critics as a pariah, he "became the butt of caricature and witticism."

At last, however, he won a few disciples to his side, and the question arose as to how they would best keep in touch. They felt the need to find a place for regular meetings, and as Manet's studio was unsuitable, they chose the spacious and comfortable **Café Guerbois**. Here, then, for some four or five years, the Impressionists and their literary friends of similar tastes regularly met to confirm each other in what some would call "the despised gospel of realism."

Manet dominated these meetings. As Théodore Duret told it:

> With his animation, his flashing wit, his sound judgment on matters of art, he gave the tone to the discussions. Moreover, as an artist who had suffered persecution, who had been expelled from the Salons, and excommunicated by the representatives of official art, he was naturally marked for the place of leadership among a group of men whose one common feature, in art and literature, was the spirit of revolt.

Later, the **Nouvelle Athènes** became the place to go, after the Guerbois was rejected as being too noisy. On the corner of the rue Frochet and the rue Pigalle, the Nouvelle Athènes had a simple white façade. One habitué remembered the café by the various odors he associated with different times of the day:

> In the morning, eggs frizzling in butter, the pungent cigarette, coffee and bad cognac; at five o'clock the vegetable smell of absinthe; after the steaming soup ascends from the kitchen and as the evening advances, the mingled smells of cigarettes, coffee, and weak beer.

Regular meetings at cafés created for many artists a substitute club, a place where they could gain a feeling of solidarity in a world that was still hostile to them. At one of these meetings, it was said, Cézanne refused to shake hands with the fastidious Manet, saying that he had not washed in a week.

Another favorite was the **Café Riche**, where artists including

Monet, Pissarro, Renoir, Caillebotte, and sometimes Stéphane Mallarmé met regularly:

> Discussions were often at a high pitch, particularly between Renoir and Caillebotte. The nervous and sarcastic Renoir with his mocking voice ... took great pleasure in exciting Caillebotte ... Conversation dealt not only with art and painting, but also with literature, politics and philosophy. A great reader ... Caillebotte would launch headlong into these debates. Renoir had armed himself by buying an encyclopedia in which he found pertinent arguments to squash his adversary ...

So observed the writer Gustave Geffroy, who had witnessed the situation first hand in the 1890s.

In *Guide de L'Etranger à Montmartre*, a tourists' guide published in 1905, the **Chat Noir** comes in for particular attention as an artists' cabaret. At the time it belonged to Aristide Bruant, and a newspaper called the *Chat Noir* was founded. Steinlen, Willette, and other artists were contributing to it; Alphonse Allais and George Auriol were responsible for the humor. The *Guide* recalls "exquisite evenings" spent in the Chat Noir when it was presided over by Rudolphe Salis, who had founded the cabaret in the first place. With two hundred people wedged into a space meant for half that many, they sat as if enthralled, receiving Salis's flattery and sarcasm in turn, listening to humorous barbs directed at—how daring it seemed at the time—the Chamber of Deputies and the Municipal Council!

A description of the clientele of the Chat Noir was provided by artist Paul Bourget:

> A fantastic mixture of writers and painters, journalists and students, workers ... without mentioning the models, *demimondaines* [call girls] and really great ladies looking for a lively scene, the whole thing presided over by a person with

an impressive appearance, with his red goatee sharpened to a point, his cocky look and impertinent mouth, giving himself the title of gentleman-cabaret keeper.

This last individual was the proprietor, Rudolphe Salis, who would move around shaking hands and greeting customers. Later in the evening he would entertain the company with his monologues, in which he would ridicule politicians, tease the bourgeois and try to shock people by making risqué comments.

What is left of the famous cafés, *café-concerts*, and cabarets of Montmartre? Some traces of the wild, uninhibited nightlife of the Butte Montmartre still remain. F. Scott Fitzgerald recalled the old days in the story "Babylon Revisited," in which the Montmartre that he remembers is "Babylon":

> After an hour he left and strolled toward Montmartre, up the rue Pigalle into the Place Blanche. The rain had stopped and there were a few people in evening clothes disembarking from taxis in front of cabarets, and cocottes prowling singly or in pairs, and many Negroes. He passed a lighted door from which issued music, and stopped with the sense of familiarity; it was Bricktop's, where he had parted with so many hours and so much money. A few doors farther on he found another ancient rendezvous and incautiously put his head inside. Immediately an eager orchestra burst into sound, a pair of professional dancers leaped to their feet and a maître d'hôtel swooped toward him, crying "Crowd just arriving, sir!" But he withdrew quickly ... up in the rue Blanche there was more light and a local, colloquial French crowd. The Poet's Cave had disappeared, but the two great mouths of the Café of Heaven and the Café of Hell still yawned—even devoured, as he watched, the meager contents of a tourist bus ...

Despite this rather unsympathetic view, traces remain of the lively artists' Montmartre

Le Bateau Lavoir, 13 Place Emile Goudeau, 75018 Paris. Métro: Abbesses. Here Picasso lived and painted *Les Demoiselles d'Avignon*. Gutted by a fire in 1970, Le Bateau has been rebuilt.

L'Elysée Montmartre, 72 boulevard de Rochechouart, 75018 Paris. Métro: Anvers. Gone are the days of La Goulue. Instead, go to admire its Belle Epoque façade.

Le Lapin Agile, 22 rue des Saules, 75018 Paris (46.06.85.87). Métro: Lamarck-Caulaincourt. Open from 9 p.m. to 2 a.m. daily. Picasso once paid for a meal here with one of his Harlequin paintings. Nowadays, the Lapin mainly caters to tourists wishing to hear old-fashioned French *chansons*.

Le Moulin Rouge, 82 boulevard de Clichy, 75018 Paris (46.06.00.19). Métro: Blanche. Le Moulin Rouge is now a high-priced nightclub, with shows at 10 p.m. and midnight, from about 450 francs per person.

For lunch and a glass of wine, you may be more attracted to:

Aux Négociants, 27 rue Lambert, 75018 Paris (46.06.15.11). Métro: Château-Rouge. Closed weekends and in August—open until 10:30 p.m. other times, Aux Négociants is identified with poets. Winner of the *meilleur pot* or "best place for wine" award.

Le Dimey, a neighborhood café on the rue des Abbesses. Le Dimey offers coffee for 5.50 and 9 francs, *café crème* 8 and 12, tea 12 and 18, soda pop 13 and 17, and wine 7 and 14 francs.

Le Sancerre, 35 rue des Abbesses, 75018 Paris (42.58.08.20). Métro: Abbesses. Open from 7 a.m. to 1:30 a.m., Le Sancerre has good simple meals, and is convenient to the Place des Abbesses.

The **Tabac de la Mairie**. Across the street from Montmartre's "*mairie*," or town hall, Le Tabac is on the corner of rues Ordener and Hermel at 28 rue Hermel, 75018 Paris (46.06.01.30). Métro: Jules Joffrin. Coffee here is just 5.50 and 10.50 francs, juice 14 and 20, mineral water 12 and 18, beer 9.50 and 19 francs, and a sandwich 15 francs.

Along with Montmartre, Montparnasse was a center for artists.

It started with the artists' colony, "La Ruche," founded in 1902 by Alfred Boucher. La Ruche offered impoverished artists a place to stay for practically nothing: an *atelier* or workshop where they could live and work cost 50 francs a year. Not only that: as Marc Chagall said, "one wasn't forced to pay!" Boucher had founded the place intending to make it a cultural center. Chagall had warm memories of La Ruche:

> Life in Montparnasse was marvellous! . . . I used to work all night. When, in a nearby *atelier*, an insulted model would start crying, when the Italians would sing, accompanying themselves on the mandolin, when Soutine would come back from the market with a bunch of chickens ready to paint them, I would stay alone in my cell made from planks, standing in front of my easel, with lighting from a miserable kerosene lamp . . . For 35 francs a trimester, I had all the conveniences.

Another artist who cherished the old times at La Ruche was Fernand Léger, who lived there from 1908 to 1909:

> La Ruche! What an extraordinary place! What wasn't there inside it? You lived however you could. You bought and sold everything at La Ruche. I remember that among others there were four Russians, nihilists. I never could understand how they managed to live in a room that was 3 square meters or how they always had vodka available.

Two cafés were especially important in the growing artists' community in Montparnasse: the **Café du Dôme** and the **Rotonde**. They faced each other across the two boulevards: the Rotonde had been there for fifteen years before the Dôme opened. Some people credited Libion, the proprietor of the Rotonde, with its success. Libion liked artists and had a liberal-minded policy towards them. He instructed his waiters to let them stay there for hours in front of an empty glass without expecting them to reorder. He even had the waiters ignore the number of croissants consumed, and would sometimes intervene himself to take away the saucers—representing money owed—by customers whom he knew to be broke. "These are the kind of people that attract attention and they will make my café famous," he said.

He was right: Picasso, Vlaminck, Matisse, and Derain frequented the Rotonde in the early 1920s. Some, like the poet Guillaume Apollinaire, complained about the artists' lack of style, remarking that "they dressed like Americans." In fact the artists appeared rather conservative: most wore bowler hats and didn't look especially bohemian.

One of the most unfortunate habitués of the two cafés was Modigliani. Although he was supported by his family—the 200 francs a month they contributed should have been enough to keep him comfortably—he wasted it on alcohol and cocaine. "A person who receives 200 francs a month to live and blows 190 of it on alcohol and drugs, lives in misery," remarked Kisling, a Polish poet living in Montparnasse at the time. Modigliani would survive to the end of the month by painting people's portraits for one franc each or for a drink.

For the artists, cafés like the **Dôme** and the **Rotonde** were indispensable as places where they could get together and exchange ideas. During World War I, Libion was approached by the authorities, who wanted him to inform for them and pass on information about his customers. Libion courageously refused, and was punished by being forced to close his café. After the Armistice, with Libion no longer the owner, the Rotonde changed. It became more and more a luxurious place for the wealthy. Artists no longer felt at home, and drifted away. The Rotonde had lost its character.

A Russian in Montparnasse at the time found **Le Parnasse**, situated between **Le Sélect** and **La Rotonde**, the most interesting café in Paris. At Le Parnasse the practice began of having artists' expositions in the cafés themselves. The **Closerie des**

Lilas, the **Petit Napolitain**, and **Le Caméléon** followed this example, helping to launch artists' careers.

Some artists' cafés which still exist, and are worth visiting, include:
Aux Artistes, 63 rue Falguière, 75015 Paris (43.22.05.39). Métro: Falguière or Pasteur. Frequented by Modigliani, Aux Artistes had not changed for years. Closed at lunchtime weekends.
La Closerie des Lilas, 171 boulevard du Montparnasse, 75006 Paris (43.26.70.50). Métro: Port-Royal. La Closerie is now beyond the means of most artists and many tourists. Try its brasserie if you must experience this historic café.
La Coupole, 102 boulevard du Montparnasse, 75014 Paris (43.20.14.20). Métro: Vavin. La Coupole is a member of the Brasserie Flo group, and well run, like all of the others. Coffee here is about 6 francs at the bar—more if you sit down.
Le Sélect, 99 boulevard du Montparnasse, 75006 Paris (45.48.38.24). Métro: Vavin. Unlike some of its larger neighbors, Le Sélect retains its historic appeal. This is a café which still has life to it: in a setting of green and cream, accented by the grey marble of the typical brass-edged tables, you can drink coffee for 6 and 15 francs, a *café crème* or beer for 10 and 24, and have a sandwich for 22 francs and up.
Some up-to-date spots outside Montparnasse may interest art lovers:
Au Petit Fer à Cheval, 30 rue Vieille-du-Temple, 75004 Paris (42.72.47.47). Métro: Saint-Paul. In the Marais, this charming turn-of-the century café has an unusual feature—a horseshoe shaped bar in grey marble! Friendly service, but this is no place for a starving artist—espresso at the bar is 12 francs after 10 p.m.
Café Beaubourg, at 43 rue Saint-Merri, 75004 Paris (48.87.63.96). Métro: Rambuteau. In this stunning, post-modern interior, coffee costs 15 francs—17 after 7 p.m.–tea, beer, and hot chocolate 25, mineral water and wine 22, a sandwich 20. From the *terrasse*, a wonderful view of the Beaubourg.

La Comédie, 11 rue de la Reynie, 75004 Paris (42.71.22.29) escapes the noise of the Place Beaubourg by its location just behind. Charming, intimate, dedicated to theater and film artists—and patronized by actors from the Théâtre du Tourtour, opposite. Coffee 6 and 9 francs.

Less interesting in decor, but handy when you're in the area is **Le Mont Lozère,** at 131 rue Saint-Martin, 75004 Paris (48.87.73.00). Close to the Pompidou Center, Le Mont Lozère charges 12 francs for coffee, 15 after 3 p.m., 20 francs for tea or hot chocolate, and 15 and 20 francs for wine and beer.

Le Cochon à L'Oreille, 15 rue Montmartre, 75001 Paris (42.36.07.56). Métro: Châtelet-Les Halles. Here are old wooden benches from the métro, and a superb, if entirely recreated, Belle Epoque-style interior, put in less than 20 years ago. Attempts to learn the prices of drinks here met with a loud and extended tirade from the head waitress. All we can say is that coffee is 8 francs if you're seated, probably 5 at the bar—and that the woman in charge has a very uncertain temper.

Le Café Marly, 93 rue de Rivoli, 75001 Paris (49.26.06.60). 8 a.m.–1:30 a.m. Metro: Palais-Royal. Paris is talking about it: the café in a former royal palace. The terrace of this café is under the colonnades of the Louvre, with a view of the statue of Louis XIV and I.M. Pei's soaring pyramid. Not easy to find: cross the street from Guimard's Art Nouveau métro entrance, Palais Royal-Musée du Louvre, and walk into the Louvre. Le Café Marly is to your right. Here you sit outside in comfortable chairs covered with the faded persimmon reminiscent of Provence. In cooler weather, the extravagant interior brings its royal palace origins to mind. Stunning views of the courtyard of the Louvre: stunning, too, the people who pass. The Café Marly is currently "in," and you see before you a parade of people who might well decorate the pages of the French *Vogue*. Or they could be emerging from elegant rue Saint-Honoré. Artists, models, actresses, designers: this is the place to see them in their native habitat. A small espresso is 16 francs, coke, orange juice, beer, and wine from 28 francs.

La Palette, 43 rue de Seine, 75006 Paris (43.26.68.15). Métro: Odéon. Open from 8 a.m. to 2 a.m.—closed Sundays. This bistro is worth seeking out if only because of its location, on the rue de Seine lined with art galleries, giving a respite from nearby boulevards Saint-Michel and Saint-Germain-des-Prés. A rather dark interior is decorated with charming efforts by aspiring artists. Coffee is 6 francs at the bar, 12 at a table; beer is 11 and 17 francs. There is not much space at the bar, so you may wish to sit down and enjoy a view of the rue de Seine along with journalists, photographers, art gallery owners—a sophisticated crowd!

La Tartine, 24 rue de Rivoli, 75004 Paris (42.72.76.85). Métro: Saint-Paul. La Tartine is more a wine bar than a café but is worth visiting for its original decor—and for the poets who go there. Details about this unusual café in "Parisians Discuss their Favorite Cafés" (see p. 133).

Vagenende, 142 boulevard Saint-Germain, 75006 Paris (43.26.68.18). Métro: Odéon. Vagenende is really a restaurant rather than a café or *brasserie*, but you can drink coffee for 17 francs and beer or mineral water for 20 during off-peak hours while admiring its authentic Art Nouveau interior. It is open until 1 a.m.

9

"Country" Cafés and Salons de Thé

"They all meet in that comparatively small number of cafés with frosted-glass windows, where a smell of country . . . always hangs in the air. They drink coffee, grog, red wine, applejack, brandy, the whole spectrum of drinks." —Georges Simenon

Here and there in Paris, within the range of the métro, you can still find cafés with the feeling of the countryside. In the afternoons men gather at these cafés. They tend to assemble in a preappointed place, all seeming to know each other. The usual handshakes and boisterous greetings start up all around, as if these habitués are following a set pattern. For these men, just being there is a well-established part of their daily routine.

André Ferré, of the Society of the Friends of Marcel Proust, described the rituals of the country café. Upon entering, "regulars" shake the proprietor's hand, flirt with the cashier, and address waiters with the familiar "*tu*" or at least by their first names. Waiters don't need to take an order—the habitués always want the same drinks.

"Even the placement and composition of the tables reflects a certain hierarchy," decided Ferré. "It is reflected even more in the specialization of different cafés themselves, and in the kind of clientele they attract. In one particular town, the elite might frequent the Café de la Promenade, while the Café de Commerce would entertain shopkeepers and only working-class people would go to the Café de la Paix. But the most important kind of specialization is the one distinguishing cafés according to the political leanings of their patrons: one is a café of the left wing, another a right-wing café, with a respectable café of devout Catholics facing a laymen's or freemasons' café." Ferré pointed out that for French people in the provinces, politics is an obsession, something like sports for the British, tulips for the Dutch, and *amor* for the Spanish. He concluded that the café "is the matrix of small political careers, and even of some great ones."

In *Village in the Vaucluse*, Harvard's Laurence Wylie observed the function of the café in a remote part of Provence. He noticed that the café tended to serve as neutral ground:

> Tourists, strangers, salesmen, any of the people coming to the village who have no access to a home may go to the café and refresh themselves. Natives wanting to meet on neutral ground to talk over a private affair can find a back table where they will be undisturbed.

Doing research in such a conservative environment was a challenge for Wylie—how could he give the villagers the tests he needed for his research without taking on the responsibilities of either host or guest? Inviting people to his home or going to their homes was out of the question. The best solution turned out to be the café.

During the hours he spent in cafés, Wylie came to realize how important they could be to social life in the village. The café was a prime source of news. Leading citizens of the town would stop by daily:

Since so many different kinds of people go to the café for different purposes and since few leave without chatting a bit with the café owner or his wife, the establishment has naturally become the unofficial information bureau of the town. All the information and misinformation gathered by the extensive network of gossip circles throughout the community is eventually funneled into the café. The town clerk spends two hours or so in the café every day. The doctor often drops in for an apéritif when he comes to town . . . With these and many other sources of information at his disposal the café owner usually knows better than anyone else in the village the news of the community.

The café became a substitute home for a group Wylie called the "Lonely Ones," a small gathering of poor adult males with nowhere else to go. They would while away the hours in the café. The café owner could not make a living from them, but depended mostly on selling drinks during the hours the café served as a recreation center for the townspeople. It was also a social center during *boules* contests, and a men's social club in the evenings before dinner. A well-established ritual determined how customers paid for their drinks:

The number of drinks consumed by each member of the circle depends on the number present, for it is customary for each to pay for a *tournée*, a round. This is a fixed procedure, but it can be varied easily through a special excuse. If someone has to leave before he has offered his round of drinks, he says, "Tomorrow will be my round." If someone has to leave before profiting from a round due him, he says, "That will be for tomorrow." When "tomorrow" comes, everyone has forgotten the postponed drink.

Drunkenness was very rare, with *pastis*, the anis-flavored drink, being the one most men ordered:

Almost the only cases of drunkenness I saw were on the rare occasions when a Lonely One had had a job, had just been paid, and consequently had had more to drink than he was accustomed to. On these occasions the Lonely One comes to life . . . He insists on setting up the house. He takes too active a part in the conversation. He never gets rolling drunk, but his conduct is embarrassing to the other men . . . If he becomes loudly or violently aggressive, they turn away from him. The *cafetier* refuses to sell him more drinks and tells him to go home to rest. Rebuffed, he goes out the door muttering to himself, and the atmosphere in the café returns to normal.

Back in Paris, foreigners are not the only ones who sometimes have difficulty adjusting to the French capital. When French people from the provinces come to Paris, they often feel that Parisians treat them with condescension. The typically Parisian sense of superiority towards people from the provinces or "provincials" is suggested in a story by Alphonse Allais, the humorist and playwright. He described an incident in a café on the boulevard Saint-Michel where he was sitting with a friend, Georges Auriol:

We sat down at a table next to which a gentleman was drinking a beer. As it was very warm, the gentleman had put his hat down on a chair.
Allais's friend, Auriol, could just make out the name and address of the hat maker: "P. Savigny, Halle Street, Tréville-sur-Meuse." Auriol, deciding to have some fun at the expense

of the provincial, asked him:

"Excuse me, sir, but you're not by any chance from Tréville-sur-Meuse?"

The surprised stranger acknowledged that he was, indeed, from that very place, as he struggled to remember who Auriol might be.

"Ah," Auriol went on, "I was sure that I couldn't have been wrong. I often go to Tréville . . . I even have a good friend there whom you might possibly know, a man named Savigny, hat maker in Halle Street."

"Do I know Savigny? We went to school together . . . I call him Paul, he calls me Ernest."

And Auriol is in the middle of one of those endless conversations about Tréville-sur-Meuse, a place he knew nothing about except the name five minutes ago. Allais continued:

"I myself, rather jealous of my friend's success, resolved to beat him at his little joke and make him envious of me. A quick look at the famous hat gave me the initials: 'E. D-H.' Two minutes spent with the telephone book were all I needed to get the full name of 'E. D.-H.'

"Very calmly, I came back to my seat and, looking at the man from Tréville, said: 'Excuse me if I'm wrong, sir, but wouldn't you be Mr. Duval-Housset?'

" 'Exactly right, Ernest Duval-Housset, at your service.'

"Certainly Mr. Duval-Housset was stunned to find himself recognized by two characters he'd never met before, but Auriol's amazement was bordering on frenzy. By what black magic had I been able to guess the name and profession of this fellow?

"I added: 'Is old Roux still the mayor of Tréville?' (I had hastily read in the telephone book this item: 'Mayor: Dr. Roux, senior.')

" 'Alas, no, we buried the poor man three months ago.'

" 'Really? He was certainly a good man, and an excellent doctor. When I became ill at Tréville, he cured me and put me back on my feet in two weeks.'

" 'They won't replace him very quickly, a man like that!'

"By now Auriol had guessed my ruse. He also went away for a while, came back soon, and our conversation continued on about Tréville-sur-Meuse and its people."

Delighted, Duval-Housset paid for the two rascals' beers, and later on insisted upon treating them to an excellent dinner. Allais and Auriol, practical jokers to the end, left quite triumphant about the success of their little game.

The writer Alphonse Allais was widely known as a wit at the time. Invited to address an audience on the subject of the theater, he opened with: "Ladies and gentlemen, I have been asked to talk to you about the theater, but I am afraid the subject will make you sad. Shakespeare is dead, Molière is dead, Racine is dead, Beaumarchais is dead, Marivaux is dead . . . and I'm not feeling too well myself."

Several cafés with a peaceful, country-like ambiance about them can be found within Paris. One of the best is **Le Temps des Cerises** at 31 rue de la Cerisaie, 75004 Paris (42.72.08.63). Métro: Bastille. It is a wonderful little find near the Bastille, a small café attracting regulars from the area. The reception is friendly, and the coffee—and selection of wines by the glass— is excellent. A delicious *menu*, or three-course lunch, is available for 68 francs on weekdays. Closed weekends and in August.

The **Café Goufre**, in front of the Senate in the Jardin du Luxembourg, is a perfect refuge from the crowds and noise of the Latin Quarter. This unusual café reminds one of a gazebo— the sort of thing you could expect to see in the spacious grounds of an elegant country house. Marble-topped tables within, green tables and chairs outside, and a great view of the Jardin wherever you choose to sit. Coffee 9 francs, tea 18. Open every day. The owner of a nearby gift shop shared her enthusiasm for this remarkable café: "I go there in the winter when nobody's around. I look out at the Jardin and I feel I'm off in—Canada!"

Chez Germaine, 30 rue Pierre-Leroux, 75007 Paris (42.73.28.34). Métro: Duroc. Closed on Sundays. Here is a small room with good food and low prices. No smoking. Tables are close together, so you might even be able to strike up a conversation with your neighbor.

Grandgousier, 17 avenue Rachel, 75018 Paris (43.87.66.12). Métro: Blanche. A quiet little place in Montmartre, near the Cimetière de Montmartre.

Marais Plus, 20 rue des Francs Bourgeois, 75003 Paris (48.87.01.40). Métro: Saint-Paul. A block from the Place des Vosges, Marais Plus has a gift shop at the front, offering colorful cards and an assortment of unusual little gift items. In the back is a room with the look of an old-fashioned farmhouse kitchen. Here you sip your coffee in a setting that is tasteful in a rustic style, with handpainted faience displayed against yellow walls and a sideboard arrayed with glowing fruit tarts. Marais Plus provides a restful change from the streets outside. Coffee is 10 francs and tea 25.

Le Peny, 3 Place de la Madeleine, 75008 Paris (42.65.06.75). Métro: Madeleine. Open daily. Despite its location on the busy Place de la Madeleine (on the opposite corner from Fauchon), Le Peny attains a relaxed country feeling, its yellow and white background colors accented by green Perrier umbrellas over the tables. Coffee is 6.50 and 14 francs, and tea a hefty 22 and 28.

Le Saint Framboise is at 142 rue des Rosiers, 93400 Saint Ouen (40.11.27.38). Métro: Clignancourt. A good escape from the noise and confusion of the large flea market that surrounds it. Prices are reasonable: coffee 7 and 9 francs, tea, Coke, or beer 13 and 17. More about this in "A Cheapskate's Guide" (see p. 117).

Tea and Sympathy

"Thank God for tea! What would the world do without tea?
How did it exist? I am glad I was not born before tea."
—Sydney Smith

What if you can't face another cup of coffee? How about tea? Paris has many *salons de thé* scattered about. Several tearooms with a country air about them exist:

Angélina, on the 3rd floor—the 4th to Americans—of the Galeries Lafayette. Métro: Chaussée d'Antin or Havre Caumartin. Angelina provides a quiet spot for tea and relaxation during a hectic day of shopping, with its cream-colored walls, glass-topped tables and Louis XV style armchairs. You may have already eaten at **Le Relais des Galeries** on the 6th floor, entering by the *libre service* sign, where a plate heaped with salad goes for 17.50 to 34 francs, depending on the size of your plate, and coffee is only 4.50 francs. If you're lucky, or late (1:45 p.m. or later), you may get one of the coveted tables by the window with a view of the old Opéra.

The original **Angélina**, at 226 rue de Rivoli, 75001 Paris (42.60.82.00), was recommended to me by a moneychanger on the rue Vivienne. Originally called Rumpelmayer's, it was founded in 1903. High-priced tea and pastries are served in a lavish setting of marble tables and red carpet. Open from 9:30 a.m. to 7 p.m., except for three weeks in August.

A Priori Thé isn't exactly a secret, but its location at 35-37 Galerie Vivienne, 75002 Paris (42.97.48.75) gives it a nice tranquillity, very tempting for the tired tourist. Métro: Bourse. Here is a charming spot for tea—the tablecloths are often topped with teapots filled with flowers. Coffee is 12 francs, a *café crème* 15, and tea 25 francs and up.

Le Bon Marché, the department store on the rue de Sèvres at the corner of the rue du Bac and near the Sèvres-Babylon métro, 75007 Paris (44.39.80.00). The world's first department store, opened in 1876, Le Bon Marché has a self-service canteen and a restaurant. Most appealing for tea is the **Côté Jardin**, open from June to September, in a courtyard setting where large white umbrellas shelter the tables. Tea here is about 22 francs.

Also on the Left Bank, **Tea and Tattered Pages** at 24 rue Mayet, 75006 Paris (40.65.94.35). Métro: Duroc or Vaneau. Tea and Tattered Pages makes tea, "brownies, fudge, and other American goodies" available. Basically a used bookstore, this is a good refuge if you are in dire need of hearing some English!

Brocco, 180 rue du Temple, 75003 Paris (42.72.19.81). Métro: République. Fight your way through the crowds around Tati, a discount clothing store on the corner, to this gem of an old-fashioned *pâtisserie* and tearoom by the Place de la République. Brocco's pastries are memorable: try the *Opéra*.

Paul Bugat, 5 boulevard Beaumarchais, 75003 Paris (48.87.89.88). Métro: Bastille. Monsieur Bugat speaks English. He and his staff welcome you at one of the highest rated *pâtisseries* in this part of Paris. Espresso is 12 francs, tea 15. The tables inside and out are filled mostly by locals. Awnings provide plenty of shade, and the *pâtisserie* is a place where you can linger to enjoy one of Bugat's delicious creations.

Ladurée, 16 rue Royale, 75008 Paris (42.60.21.79). Métro: Madeleine or Concorde. Exactly the sort of place you wish your grandmother had taken you to. Elegant wood panelling, mirrors, and charm. Open from 8:30 a.m. to 7 p.m., this *salon de thé* has ambiance that more than justifies the prices—18 francs for coffee, 22 for tea.

Thé au Fil, 80 rue Montmartre, 75002 Paris (42.36.95.49). In this cheerful green and yellow *salon de thé*, good smells of desserts and *plats* waft up from the kitchen. Everything is made fresh daily. Coffee 11 francs, tea 22.

In the 9th arrondissement, on the little street behind

Fauchon on the Place de la Madeleine are some good *salons de thé*:

Chiba, an excellent *pâtisserie* and tearoom, at 28 rue Vignon, 75009 Paris (47.42.01.24). Métro: Madeleine. In this quiet little spot, away from noisy Place de la Madeleine, coffee is 9 francs, tea 18, and a variety of good pastries are about 20 francs apiece. Here a Parisienne scornfully referred to Fauchon as a *"grand surface de luxe,"* meaning that it had become too large an operation. In any case, Chiba's prices are gentler than Fauchon's.

Tarte Julie, 12 rue Vignon, 75009 Paris (47.42.96.34). Métro: Madeleine. Tarte Julie is part of a chain that makes tasty pastries and complete lunches. In an attractive tearoom with cream-colored walls, you can enjoy coffee at 9 francs, tea for 16 and Coke for 14. A good-sized slice of pie or *tarte* will be 24 to 28 francs. Take-out is available.

Le Loir dans la Théière, 3 rue des Rosiers, 75004 Paris (42.72.90.61). Métro: Saint-Paul. Situated in an unusually attractive quarter, Le Loir has a pleasant country atmosphere. Lunch will cost from 80 to 100 francs.

10

From the Other Side of the Counter

"We'll teach you to drink deep ere you depart."—Shakespeare

All café-goers must sometimes wonder about the man and woman behind the counter. What have they seen, heard, and learned in many years of dealing with the public, often with a select group of regulars who tell them everything about their lives?

In an interview in the magazine *Reflets*, Lucien Delorme, a café proprietor from the Basque area of southwestern France, talked about "a human warmth, an understanding, a humanity which doesn't show up in any similar form of business" yet is to be found in cafés. He explained why people go to cafés: "The fellow who comes into a café is depressed, he's lost, and the first contact is a smile, it's a certain friendliness, a greeting that you want." Delorme went on to explain that there is a ritual going on behind what one observes in a café: the behavior of the barman is conditioned by what he feels the clients need:

The fellow feels suddenly at ease, the individual is taken care of, he doesn't feel alone any more, if he wants to talk, he talks, and if he doesn't, well . . . it's true that our occupations are a bit feverish or rushed, and the waiter doesn't perhaps have time to come and concern himself with the mental health of the customer, but if he has just a little bit of time he asks him something and the opening is made . . . there is talk, there is dialogue between them and it's good.

Alexandre Guini, a successful Parisian *cafetier* or proprietor of a café, emphasized the importance of keeping an eye on the client:

You must know how to make yourself respected by the customer, you must not let people go, talk too loudly, because at that moment they are going to be troublesome to the person beside them. You have to watch a certain customer, the type who when he begins to drink just a little bit becomes bad. You have to know how to stop the client at a certain moment, to say to him no, stop, for you it's finished, you have drunk enough, you're not drinking any more, and all that . . . You have to do it with kindness, with tact . . . A certain type of personality is necessary for this. You don't have to be two meters tall but you have to know how to impose your will, always with kindness. Especially you must never try to get close to the customer . . . To use the familiar "*tu*" with him, that's a catastrophe. As for me, I always say when I hear a proprietor of a café calling his client "*tu*" . . . that makes me mad because it's a lack of deference towards the client. A certain physical presence is necessary.

Explaining what he means by a physical presence, Guini observed that sometimes, not every day but once in a while, it might become necessary to expel a customer from the café:

When it is necessary to throw somebody out, you have to do it nicely, with politeness, but it's still necessary, so you have to roll up your sleeves and then, tell him to leave . . . I'm 1.78 metres in height, and weigh about a hundred and ten kilos [about 250 pounds] . . . I have in front of me what they call a "*durillon de comptoir*"—a fairly prominent stomach— I have a big moustache and hair a bit salt and pepper in color, and also I have a smile which women used to call enchanting. . . . That, in your opinion, is the prototype of a good patron of a café. Ah, maybe it's my look, but I know that for me it's worked, nobody has lacked respect and I've demanded that customers show respect for me too.

One of the best accounts of life behind the bar was related by a former barman, Jimmie Charters. In *This Must Be the Place*, he recalled working as a barman in Montparnasse. Along with comments about the Montparnasse scene in the 1920s— he said he had never been in a madhouse before he went to Montmartre, had never seen people drink to get drunk and had "never seen artists, writers, nobles, American sailors and doubtful women mingle on equal terms without reserve"—Charters discussed the qualities of a good barman. He, too, maintained that to be successful, a barman had to maintain a certain distance from his customers:

I have always believed success behind the bar comes from an ability to understand the man or woman I am serving, to enter into his joys or woes, make him feel the need of me as a person rather than as a servant. And yet—and this is so important—to keep my place. It is sometimes hard to draw the line. There are men I have addressed as "Mister" for ten years, and probably will for another ten years, whom I know better than their best friends.

Charters quoted from a letter written to him by Samuel Putnam, an author and editor who knew Montparnasse in the 1920s and 1930s. Putnam remembered Jimmy in action:

> I can see Jimmie yet, reaching across the bar, gentle like, to put an obstreperous customer to sleep . . . then, one hand on the bar and he's across, picking the guy up, dusting him off, and sending him home in a taxi—and paying his fare! That was Jimmie. I often wondered how he made any money.

Charters remembered the **Dôme** as a focal point for both English people and Americans in Paris in the 1920s. People would go there in the morning to breakfast on croissants and coffee. Then on to the day's activities: artists might attend classes, writers return to their apartments to work, or go around Paris with friends. In the afternoon they would be back at the Dôme drinking an *apéritif* as a prelude to the evening, "first because French housing laws do not permit *any* noise after ten o'clock, and secondly because it was so much more economical to meet your friends in a bar where each paid for his own drink."

Concerning the art of bartending, Charters stressed the importance of preventing fights. He said he could usually "smell" a fight coming on, and would do his utmost to make sure that it didn't take place, by telling jokes or by giving free drinks to the would-be combatants. Usually the free drink worked. He found fights between women much harder to deal with than among men: "When I see one of these coming on I first remove all the loose objects from the bar, such as ashtrays, glasses, bottles, and plates. If things begin to get rough I threaten to call the police, for women are far more afraid of the cops than are men."

He'd make an effort to talk with customers who seemed lonely or in need of a little conversation with someone. He would get them to meet others at the bar without actually making a formal introduction:

Most people won't admit they are lonely, especially the over-reserved English people, who nevertheless welcome conversation with someone else. As I am serving them they will talk to me because they know me. When I have two such persons in the bar I usually manage to stand between them. First I talk to one and then I talk to the other, always trying to make them laugh at the same time. Soon they are talking to each other and I go away.

One of the "perks" of the barman's trade can be the opportunity to meet celebrities. Charters served drinks to many of the celebrated writers of the time. One was Sinclair Lewis, whom he didn't particularly like: "His red head could usually be seen at the Dôme amid a group of the curious. He came into my bar once or twice, but he was not friendly to barmen. In fact he was not friendly to Montparnasse, saying that most of us were a crowd of useless drunks."

A more congenial couple were "Mike" and "Brett," the hero and heroine of Hemingway's *The Sun Also Rises*. According to Charters, everybody in the quarter knew them. Charters liked both of them, particularly "Mike," to whom he gave credit and sympathy after his breakup with "Brett." He remembers a story about "Mike" having said to Ernest Hemingway: "I got in a terrible fight about you yesterday. I was in the H—bar and I heard two men talking about you. I couldn't hear what they were saying, but I kept hearing the name Ernest Hemingway. So I went over to them and I said, 'Are you friends of Ernest Hemingway?' And they said, 'No.' So I socked them both!"

Charters had not known Oscar Wilde, but had heard many stories about the English playwright from those who had. One such story was told to him by the writer Frank Harris. He related that he was crossing the Pont Neuf with a French poetess who had the reputation of being the ugliest woman in Paris. To Wilde, appearances mattered: many of his best lines in *The Importance of Being Earnest* are about the necessity of looking just right. In the distance Harris saw Wilde approaching—now there was no way of avoiding him:

"I have heard of you," said the actress, when Wilde was introduced to her.
"And I of you, Madame," he replied.
"I have no doubt," she said. "I am known for my face—the ugliest in Paris."
Wilde made a gallant gesture and a bow.
"In the world, Madame!" he replied.

In his evaluation of the years on the other side of the counter, Charters agreed with most other barmen and even with Simenon's Inspector Maigret about what people look for in a café or bar. They are seeking a bright, cheery atmosphere, where they can meet people and have a good time. Charters didn't think decorations or food were particularly important—remember he was from England, not France—but believed that prices should be kept high so that a place could be kept reasonably exclusive.

Some terms which a barman—or frequent customer—might use in a café are:

cadavre (cadaver)—an empty bottle
gros rouge qui tache (coarse red which stains)—ordinary wine with a high alcoholic content
kilo—a liter of wine
notaire du coin (local notary public)—an indirect way of saying "I'm going to the bar."
Staline (Stalin)—after the Russian revolution, a glass of ordinary red wine.

In my own conversations with barmen and proprietors of cafés, I have noticed certain characteristics that many of them seem to share. Most have cheerful, upbeat personalities—if they get depressed, they don't show it. Contact with the public must become trying at times, but the people who serve up the coffee are adept at chatting with customers, trying to make them feel at home, so that this will be the café they return to. The large, rather chilly interior of the **Café du Dôme**, for example, was noticeably improved by the friendliness of Robert, the barman who was on duty when I visited. He not only supplied me with a cup of good espresso, he threw in a sample of a free cocktail–mostly lemonade–and reminisced about his twenty-three years on the job.

At **Au Drapeau**, near the Bastille, I learned from the proprietor why the telephone numbers of some cafés are unlisted: "Some idiot calls up early on a Sunday," he said, "wondering if we're open–we're not–and it wakes me up." Evidently there are still proprietors who live on the premises.

Even in a large city like Paris, it is not unheard of for people to develop a friendly relationship with the owner of their local café. Terry, the architect mentioned in Chapter 12, has said that the proprietors of the small café beside his apartment building sometimes do favors for customers, such as keeping an item that has been delivered for them until they can get home, often late in the day. Marie Louise, a teacher who likes to stop at **Au Béranger**, near the République, mentioned that the proprietor occasionally treats her and her friends to free cups of coffee.

Hoping for some recommendations of outstanding cafés from a cafetier himself, I spoke to Monsieur Vimard, proprietor of **Le Temps des Cerises**. It was almost the end of July: he and his wife were about to close the café, preparing to go on vacation to the Lot region in the Southwest, and I wanted some ideas about where a person who remained in Paris might go in August. I could have anticipated his answer: "The best café in Paris is closed in August," he said. He might be right.

The Cafés of Paris

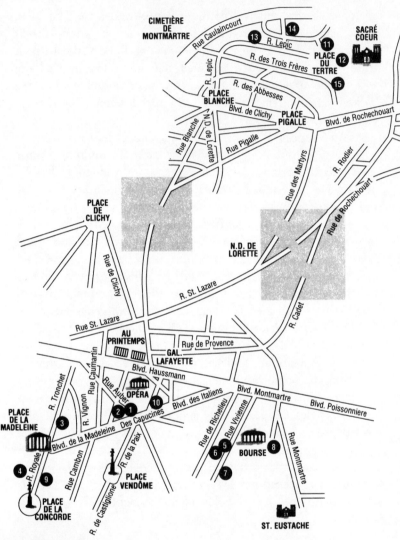

Convenient Cafés

1. Cafe de la Paix, 12 bd. des Capucines
2. L' Entr'acte, 1 rue Auber
3. Fauchon, 30 Place de la Madeleine
4. Espace Café Bleu, 15 rue du fbg St. Honoré
5. Le Vaudeville, 29 rue Vivienne
6. Riva Sandwich, 2 rue des Colonnes
7. L' Aiglon, 12 rue Vivienne
8. Gallopin, 40 r. N. D. des Victoires
9. Ladurée, 16 rue Royale
10. Le Grain de Café, 4 Place de l' Opera
11. La Mère Catherine, 6 Place du Tertre
12. Au Clairon des Chasseurs, 3 Place du Tertre
13. La Crêpe à Pic, 35 r. Lepic
14. La Maison Rose, 2 r. de l' Abreuvoir
15. Le Carrousel, 8 r. des Trois Frères

11

A Cheapskate's Guide to Cafés:
All Around Paris

"Economy is the art of making the most of life. The love of economy is the root of all virtue."—George Bernard Shaw

W hat is the cheapest place for a cup of coffee in Paris? Surprisingly enough, it's in a very fashionable setting, the elegant 8th arrondissement. Right next to the exclusive Prince of Wales and George V hotels, the American Cathedral offers free coffee every Sunday after the 11 a.m. service. In good weather, you stand outside in a Gothic Revival courtyard, flanked by flowering shrubs and potted plants. Over the years, I have gone to church there with George and Barbara Bush, Olivia de Havilland, and a number of American ambassadors to Paris: not all of them have shown up at coffee hour after the service, unfortunately, but there are enough sparkling personalities present to brighten even a dull Sunday morning! More meaningful than going to church with politicians and movie stars have been the friends in Paris met over coffee at coffee hour. If you go to a church or temple at home, consider continuing to do so as a tourist: there is nothing that will make you feel so much at home and give you such a sense of community in a foreign city.

If you lack the chutzpah for the American Cathedral or it isn't Sunday, one of the best bets for a reasonably priced cup of coffee is a department store. Try the elegant department stores on the boulevard Haussmann: **Galeries Lafayette**, at 40 boulevard Haussmann, 75009 Paris (42.82.34.56) is a particular treasure for the bargain-hunting tourist. Métro: Chaussée d'Antin. Prices in the sixth-floor cafeteria are kept deliberately low to attract shoppers. You can go through the line and get a salad lunch for from 18 to 35 francs, depending on the size of plate you choose to pile your salads and cold cuts on. A hard roll of good French bread will run about 2 francs, and excellent coffee is available for 5.80 francs. One of the best aspects about this self-service cafeteria is the view: a little patience or the willingness to go at off peak hours and you are rewarded with a booth from which you can look down to a panoramic view of the boulevard, including Charles Garnier's magnificent Opéra.

The area of the department stores can be a fruitful hunting ground for other types of quick snacks. Go into the **Marks and Spencer** at 35 boulevard Haussmann across the street from the big department store **Au Printemps**. Métro: Havre-Caumartin. You may be surprised to find it full of French people who have developed a taste for English specialities: scones, lemon butter, Scottish smoked salmon, and an outstanding variety of teas. Packaged sandwiches and soft drinks are available here at a minimal price, useful if you're hungry or thirsty and don't have time to stop for a regular lunch elsewhere. Walking from the department stores to the Opéra, you pass boutiques that may be worth a closer look—especially during the summer sales.

Between the Galeries Lafayette, at 40 boulevard Haussmann and Au Printemps at 64 boulevard Haussmann is a **Monoprix**—

but what a Monoprix! Normally considered the refuge of the penny pincher, or a French version of the five-and-dime, this has to be one of the most elegant supermarkets you will ever see. A great place for last-minute gift shopping—items purchased in supermarkets are usually free of the 17 to 33 percent luxury tax that makes consumer goods so costly in France—this Monoprix also has a coffee bar, a champagne bar, a counter specializing in smoked salmon ... need I go on? The coffee bar, **Café Malongo**, offers several varieties of coffee, all at attractive prices from 6 to 20 francs. Seating is available at the bar, but at peak hours coffee drinkers crowd around, awaiting their caffeine from the friendly looking waitresses behind the bar. Tea is between 12 and 15 francs. The bar stools are not especially comfortable, but this "café" offers an air-conditioned place to pause from shopping while sipping good coffee. In summer, iced tea is available—the iced coffee is coffee whipped to a froth and served with ice.

Normally I try to avoid chains, preferring to see what "Mom and Pop" can come up with. **Lina's Sandwiches** is an exception: very clean and bright, with reasonably priced food and drink, Lina's is scattered over the city:

50 rue Etienne Marcel, 75002 Paris (42.21.16.14). Métro: Etienne Marcel.

27 rue Saint-Sulpice, 75006 Paris (43.29.14.14), near Saint-Sulpice and the Jardin du Luxembourg. Métro: Saint-Sulpice.

8 rue Marbeuf, 75008 Paris (47.23.92.33) Métro: Alma-Marceau.

At **Lina's**, you will pay 6 francs for coffee, 8 for mineral water, 10 for soda, 18 for freshly squeezed juices, 15 for wine or beer, and 18 francs on up for a well-made sandwich. Newspapers, including the *International Herald Tribune*, are available to read.

119

Fashionable Paris

In the chic 1st arrondissement, near the Louvre, is the **Louvre des Antiquaires**—a source for the serious antique buyer and for those who like to admire the *crème de la crème*. You want an authentic Renaissance crossbow? Someone here has one. Magnificent, very specialized collections–many of museum quality–are for sale. On the top floor near the back is a small but pleasant café, the Marengo, where you can overhear dealers discussing trends in Lalique crystal or venerable manuscripts. Coffee is only 6.50 francs, Italian espresso 8, and other drinks are equally reasonable. Best of all, you can indulge in a Häagen-Dazs ice cream while resting in air-conditioned comfort. There are clean washrooms, too.

One summer in Paris we found ourselves spending much of our free time at **Fauchon**, at 26 Place de la Madeleine, in the 8th arrondissement. Métro: Madeleine. Normally Fauchon is considered big-splurge territory, a place for the budget-conscious tourist to avoid. Its lavish display of exquisitely garnished food is one of the sights of Paris. Many Parisians pause for a look outside without a thought of going in. Yet Fauchon is a great place for a coffee break! The downstairs cafeteria of the gift shop side of Fauchon–on the north side of the Place de la Madeleine (look for gift boxes in the show windows)—has a curving staircase leading down to one of the most restful, congenial places you'll find for a low-priced cup of coffee. Six francs buys you a delicious espresso and the right to sit down at a table—there is no price difference here between standing and sitting. With your coffee, you receive a distinctive silver and black sachet of sugar, marked with the Fauchon "F" and a little *tablette* of chocolate, similarly marked, at no extra charge. (Upstairs these chocolates and sugar are gift boxed for sale if you want to take away a souvenir of your visit.)

Other amenities at Fauchon's cafeteria include mainstream French newspapers, *Le Figaro* and *Le Monde*, and clean restrooms—not always the easiest thing to find in a capital city. The food at Fauchon's cafeteria is high-priced. But the boutique above the cafeteria is a wonderful place to browse and buy little gifts to take home: one of the best buys we have found is the syrup in exotic flavors: mango (*mangue*), passion fruit (*fruit de la passion*) and others not readily available in Britain or the U.S. The staff are courteous and multilingual.

Au Bon Marché, at 38 rue de Sèvres, 75007 Paris (45.49.21.22). Métro: Sèvres-Babylone. This is the Left Bank version of the large department stores. Reasonably priced food and drink is available there, particularly in its self-service area, from 11:30 a.m. to 3 p.m., Monday to Saturday. White tables and chairs in gleaming red, yellow, and blue set off a clean and cheerful place for lunch. A plate of salad is 18 francs, coffee 5, a small carafe of wine 11 francs, pastries about 20 francs—many of them large enough for two people to share. Near this cafeteria is the **Galerie des Antiquaires**, with an outstanding selection of antiques–not all of them too much of a challenge to take home with you. One dealer specialized in vintage postcards, for example. I had the memorable experience of finding two featuring the young Charles Lindbergh, made soon after his historic fight.

The Marais

The 4th arrondissement or the Marais has become very fashionable, almost what the 6th used to be. Some modest places offer reasonably priced food and drinks because they cater to ordinary people who live and work nearby:

Bar 14, 14 rue de Bretagne, 75003 Paris, is on the edge of the Marais. Métro: Temple. It is very simple—a typical workingman's bar, in the shopping district of the rue de Bretagne. Light green walls, round metal tables and wooden chairs— no glamor here, but friendly service and low prices. Coffee is from 4.50 to 6.50 francs, beer 9 to 15.

Le Petit Gavroche, 15 rue Sainte-Croix-de-la-Bretonnerie, 75004 Paris (48.87.74.26). Near métro St. Paul or Hôtel de Ville and located in the Marais, Le Petit Gavroche provides food and drink at reasonable prices but maintains its image as a worker's bar. Leave your *Wall Street Journal* or *Financial Times* at the hotel!

On the way home from the BHV—a no nonsense department store specializing in supplies for the do-it-yourself types—I ran into **Le Bistrot Gourmand**, a "bar-restaurant" at 1 rue DuPuis, in the 3rd arrondissement (42.74.64.95). Métro: République or Temple. On Friday and Saturday evenings, salads are featured—they run from 48 to 65 francs, not bad for this quiet little street near the République. There's an outstandingly friendly welcome. Coffee 6 and 11 francs.

Cafés near the Opéra at the Bastille have to charge relatively high prices to survive in what has become a high-rent district. To get better value for your money, go a short distance from the Place. Walk down the rue du Faubourg St. Antoine to the rue de Charonne. Here you'll find the **Pause Café**, at 41 rue de Charonne 75011 Paris (48.06.80.33), where the ambiance is exceptionally friendly and the prices fair: coffee 5.80 and 10 francs. Or try the nearby **Bistrot du Peintre** at 116 avenue Ledru-Rollin, (47.00.34.39). You'll be delighted by its Art Nouveau interior, dating from 1900, and by the efficient service and good food.

On the Place, the **Café Le Bastille**, at 8 Place de la Bastille, 75011 Paris (43.07.79.95), has coffee available for 6 and 14 francs, a double 10.60 and 24 francs, *café crème* 6 and 12, hot chocolate 12 and 22, tea 13 and 20, beer 9.80 and 18, wine 5.50 and 16, and sandwiches 17 francs and up. Plates of lunch go for around 50 francs, with the old standards like *croque monsieur* at 25. Häagen-Dazs ice cream is from 32 francs for two scoops to considerably more for a sundae. Le Bastille has yellow and brown wicker chairs, a red tiled floor—and a friendly barman behind the modern zinc bar.

Its next-door neighbor, **La Brasserie Bastille**, charges 12 francs for coffee on the terrace, 22 for tea, and 18 for most cold drinks, including soft drinks and mineral water. Both cafés have a great view of the square.

The Place des Vosges, in the 4th arrondissement, attracts tourists and Parisians by its beauty and historic associations. Cafés and restaurants right on the Place are understandably expensive: the **Café Martini** is a few feet away at 11 rue Pas de la Mule, 75004 Paris (42.77.05.04). Métro: Bastille. The Café Martini serves coffee for 6 and 10 francs, beer for 12 and 15. Generally filled with a lively crowd, the café has an attractive old-style wooden façade featuring the name conspicuously lettered in gold.

Au Gamin de Paris, 49 rue Vieille du Temple, 75004 Paris (42.78.97.24). Métro: Hôtel de Ville or Rambuteau. A warm and inviting restaurant-bar, Au Gamin is on the corner of the rue Vieille du Temple and rue des Blancs Manteaux, in the 4th arrondissement. Coffee is 5.50 and 11 francs, tea 14, and a glass of wine 14. Prices rise 30 percent after 10 p.m. Au Gamin makes a variety of Spanish *tapas*, or hors d'oeuvres, available.

La Locandiera Bar in the Marais, is at 21 rue de Turenne 75004 Paris (40.27.93.10). Métro: Chemin Vert or Bastille. La Locandiera has food and drink at reasonable prices: coffee 6 and 8 francs, cappuccino 12 and 14, and tea 11 and 13, soda and wine 13 and up, sandwiches 20 francs and up, and one-plate lunches for 38 francs and up. Sleekly modern in black and white, La Locandiera is open from 8:30 a.m. to 7:30 p.m.

Great Views

Across from the Hôtel de Ville, with a partial view of Notre Dame across the river, is the **Paris Midi**, at 2 quai de Gesvres, 75004 Paris (42.72.00.04). Métro: Hôtel de Ville. Coffee under these red and gold awnings is 10 francs, tea and soda 20, mineral water 18, beer 20 francs and up, and wine 19 francs and up. A 3-franc surcharge is added after 10 p.m.

Au Vieux Châtelet, 1 Place du Châtelet, 75001 Paris (42.33.79.27). Métro: Châtelet. From here you can look across the Seine at the Conciergerie, where Marie Antoinette was imprisoned during the French Revolution. Here coffee is 5 and 10 francs, juice 15 and 20, soda 14 and 20, beer 9.50 and 15, and a sandwich 15 francs.

Near the cathedral of Notre Dame, there are three cafés. **Café Notre Dame**, at 21 Quai Montebello (43.54.19.71) offers basic espresso at 5.50 and 13 francs. On the opposite side at **Aux Tours de Notre Dame**, 23 rue Arcole, 75004 Paris (43.25.97.27), the price is 6 and 14 francs. Métro: Hôtel de Ville or Cité. Both cafés offer splendid views of the cathedral.

Le Quasimodo Notre-Dame, 11 rue d'Arcole, 75004 Paris is only a block away from the cathedral. Here you can drink coffee for 5.80 and 10 francs, tea for 11 and 19, while recalling Victor Hugo's *The Hunchback of Notre Dame*. Le Quasimodo is noisy yet appealing with its burgundy and gold decor.

The best perspective of all is from the **La Samaritaine** department store, 19 rue de la Monnaie, 75001 Paris (40.41.20.20). Métro: Pont-Neuf. Across the river from the Square du Vert Galant on the Ile de la Cité, La Samaritaine is located right next to the métro. Here you have a stunning view of Paris, from either the restaurant or the bar section. If you choose the bar section you can limit yourself to coffee and enjoy an outstanding look at the city for only 10 francs.

Ile Saint-Louis

On the ultra-chic Ile Saint-Louis, **Le Saint Régis** is at 6 rue Jean du Bellay 75004 Paris (43.54.59.41). Métro: Pont Marie. Le Saint Régis serves coffee for 6 and 11.50 francs, Coke and Orangina for

21, mineral water, beer, and wines from 19 francs and up. Le Saint Régis has attractive square tables, red banquettes, and black bentwood chairs.

At **Au Lys d'Argent**, at 90 rue Saint-Louis en l'Ile 75004 Paris (46.33.56.13) coffee is 10 francs, *café crème* and wine 16, tea 22, viennese coffee 26 francs. This is a charming café, with yellow walls, small, marble-topped tables, and chairs of green and wicker.

A favorite on the Ile Saint-Louis is **Le Lutetia**, at 33 quai de Bourbon 75004 Paris (43.54.11.71). Métro: Pont Marie. Coffee is 11 francs, *café crème*, tea, or hot chocolate 21, and wine, beer, and sandwiches start at 21 francs. The colors are hunter green, or as the French call it, *vert wagon*, the traditional green used on train cars, complemented by chairs in black and tan, cream walls, and lace curtains.

Centre Pompidou

Near the **Pompidou Center**, or Beaubourg, try the **Café Beaubourg**, at 43 rue Saint-Merri, 75004 Paris (48.87.63.96). Métro: Rambuteau. It can't be called inexpensive, with coffee 16 francs (18 after 7:00 p.m.), *café crème*, hot chocolate, and tea 26 francs, wine and beer beginning at 25 francs, and sandwiches 20 francs. Still, the stunning post-modern decor makes this café worth a stop. With all of the nightlife on the Place Georges Pompidou, you generally get a free *spectacle*—or entertainment—thrown in.

Le Cavalier Bleu, nearby on the corner of rue Rambuteau and rue Saint-Martin, is a more conventional café—still, coffee 5.80 and 10 francs, tea and fruit juice 22, with 3 francs added *après 12 heures.*"

An inexpensive alternative is the **Duchesne Boulangerie-Caféteria** at 149 rue Saint-Martin (42.72.64.60). But far more appealing is the attractive lively **Comédie** at 11 rue de la Reynie, 75004 Paris (42.71.22.29). Go there and you may meet some of the actors who work at the theater across the street.

The Left Bank

In the 5th arrondissement, near the Jardin du Luxembourg—the Jardin is always worth strolling in—is:

Au Départ, 1 rue Gay-Lussac, 75005 Paris (46.34.63.98). Métro: Luxembourg. Coffee is 5.50 and 10 francs. Au Départ won't win any prizes for decor—the look is shiny, with a brass-colored bar and shiny pink surfaces abounding. A pinball machine or *flipper* provides background noise. In *My Life of Absurdity*, African-American writer Chester Himes described coming here in the mornings to write. You'll enjoy the location, across from the Jardin du Luxembourg. Ford Madox Ford described this district as "a grey, very quiet quarter with the gardens of the Luxembourg like a great green jewel on its breast."

In the chic 6th arrondissement, you may wish to have coffee at the historic **Deux Magots**, opposite the church of Saint-Germain-des-Prés. Métro: Saint-Germain-des-Prés. Because of its fashionable location and association with the "greats" of twentieth-century American and French literature (see Chapters 1 and 2), the Deux Magots can get away with charging its customers 22 francs for coffee. If you don't want to pay those sorts of prices, do as my husband and I often do when in the area: shop for sandwiches, cold cuts, quiche, cheese, fruit, or pastries and soft drinks at the **Monoprix** across the street. Then carry your picnic lunch to the Square Louis Prache right beside the church. A recent lunch included a generous-sized baguette with ham, a can of Fanta *citron* lemonade, and a bunch of the largest, most delicious black cherries I had ever seen. Delicious—and less than 20 francs per person.

If you still want coffee, there's no reason to splurge at the Deux Magots. A few yards away under the red and gold awnings of the **Bonaparte**, coffee is available for 6.50, 15 or 18 francs depending on whether you choose to stand at the bar or sit inside or on the terrace.

La Coupole, at 102 boulevard de Montparnasse, 75014 Paris (43.20.14.20). Métro: Vavin. La Coupole must be one of the few remaining famous cafés where coffee is still available at the bar for 6 francs. Details in "American Cafés," p. 12.

The **Bar du Marché** has been attracting attention. It has a good location—75 rue de Seine, 75006 Paris, near the rue de Buci market, but that's about all. When we ordered coffee at the bar, the barman tried to foist large *café-crèmes* on us— at 5:45 p.m.! The service stopped just short of being surly. He next tried to discourage us from sitting at the bar: "because people will be coming in to eat." Coffee is 6 and 11 francs.

In the same neighborhood, a real "find" is the **Bar de L'Institut**, at 21 rue de Seine (43.26.98.75), just around the corner from Oscar Wilde's hotel at 13 rue des Beaux-Arts. Métro: Saint-Germain-des-Prés. The Bar de L'Institut is cozy and intimate, with dark beams against a light plaster ceiling, wood panelling and bar. Its reasonable prices are appropriate for a café catering to the students and faculty of the Sorbonne: coffee is 5.50 and 7 francs, soda 15 and 17, beer 11 and 15, and a sandwich 18 francs. The *Institut* in the Bar's name is a reference to the nearby Institut de France, which incorporates the Académie Française as well as the Académies of Sciences, Beaux-Arts, Sciences Morales and Politiques, and Inscriptions and Belles Lettres.

Near the Eiffel Tower in the 7th Arrondissement

Best buys don't include a view of the tower, unfortunately, but you'll be only a short walk away if you try:

Relais de la Tour, 27 avenue de la Bourdonnais, 75007 Paris (47.05.44.93). Métro: Pont de l'Alma. Coffee goes for 6 and 11 francs, hot chocolate for 7.50, tea 11 and 18, wine 14 and 15, and beer for 9.50 and 16 francs. The Relais has a pleasant interior, with the smells of good cooking wafting up from the kitchen to you as you stand by the brass bar looking at the oak-panelled walls and contemporary mural of the Eiffel Tower.

Its neighbor **Le Royal Tour** is on the corner of avenue Bourdonnais and rue de Montessey, 75007 Paris (47.05.04.54). Métro: Champ de Mars or Pont de l'Alma. Le Royal Tour has a large *terrasse* and offers coffee at 6 and 11 francs.

For "starvation" budgets, there's **Eiffel Fast Food**, 26 rue de Montessey, with soft drinks at 10 francs, coffee 8.

If, on the other hand, you feel like splurging, try **Chez Francis**, across the river at 7 Place de l'Alma, 75008 Paris (47.23.39.53), for one of the best views in the city of the Eiffel Tower. Coffee 20 francs.

In the Eiffel Tower itself, at the first level—a climb costs 14 francs, a ride 20—there's **Le Buffet**, with coffee at 7 francs, or the more glamorous **Altitude 95**, with coffee at 12 francs. Meals at Altitude include an elevator ticket with no waiting in line. Altitude 95, Tour Eiffel 75007 Paris (45.55.00.21).

Pigalle

In the notorious red light district Pigalle, one of the best choices in a sleazy area is **Batifol Blanche**, at 3 Place Blanche, 75009 Paris (48.74.39.37). Métro: Blanche. Open daily, from 11 a.m. to midnight, this "Batifol"—part of a chain—is directly opposite the **Moulin Rouge**. It has a classy look, with the dark wood bar and wainscotting contrasting with cream walls, hung with framed black-and-white photos of celebrities. Since Batifol is a restaurant rather than a café, you should stand at the bar if you just want a drink. Here coffee is 7 francs, Coke 18, tea or beer 16.50, and wine 11 francs and up. A *plat* or plate of food is 54 or 70 francs, and a assortment of cheeses 21 francs.

The République

On the **Place de la République** are two elegant *brasseries* mentioned in "Maigret's Cafés," the **Relais d'Eguisheim** and the **Thermomètre** (see p. 42). Métro: République. Besides these, there are immensely popular *brasseries* facing the statue.

Captain Thenint is gone—it has been swallowed up by a Tex-Mex chain. But at **Le Royal République**, 11 Place de la République 75003 Paris (42.72.31.44), coffee is 6 and 12 francs and as the sign says, *Service continu*. Open early and late. After 10 p.m. prices rise by 3.50 francs.

La Taverne Bar Belge, nearby at 5 Place de la République, 75003 Paris (42.78.50.86), offers coffee for 7 and 12.50 francs, beer starting at 12 and 18, juice for 19 and 26, soda 19 and 21.50, mineral water 15 and 20, a sandwich for 18 francs and a *croque monsieur* for 30.50 francs.

Montmartre

In the crowded, touristy area of Montmartre, you may want to avoid the crowds at the Place du Tertre or in front of Sacré Coeur and look a bit farther down the slopes for refreshment. Several possibilities:

Le Balto, 58 rue Custine, 75018 Paris (46.06.17.88). Métro: Château Rouge. Le Balto is relatively modern, with its zinc bar and pinball machines. Located opposite a *boulangerie-confiserie*, Le Balto is completely lacking in glamor, but has a pleasant neighborhood feeling to it—the friendly service and low prices more than compensate for a slight shabbiness in the decor. Coffee is 5.20 and 10, hot chocolate 7 and 10, tea 13 and 17, beer 7 and 19, and wine 5 and 14 francs, with a ham sandwich going for 15 francs. Try to get these prices in the Place du Tertre!

Bistro des Abbesses, 36 rue les Abbesses, 75018 Paris. Métro: Abbesses. Here is a copper bar, a pinball machine, and relaxing ambiance, even if there aren't many places to sit. There are no pretensions about this neighborhood bistro, serving coffee at 5 and 7 francs, *café crème* and hot chocolate at 6 and 8, and tea at 5 and 12. Closed from August 15 to August 25.

La Crêpe à Pic, 35 rue Lepic, 75018 Paris (42.55.95.95). Métro: Lamarck Caulaincourt. This is one of the more charming places in the area. Very clean, with bright tablecloths giving a look of Provence, La Crêpe offers coffee at 9 francs, tea 12, hot chocolate and Coke 15, milk 12, half a carafe of wine 20. Open from 12 to 3 p.m. and 5 to 11. If all you want is a drink and a snack, avoid the noon rush and the dinner hour.

Le Gavroche, at 22 rue Hermel, 75018 Paris (46.06.40.63), is another possibility. Métro: Jules Joffrin. Situated on the corner of the rue Hermel and the rue Ramey, Le Gavroche is a small café, with lace curtains, ochre walls—and a formica bar. But we like the prices: coffee 5 and 8 francs, *café crème* 7 and 9, a large *café crème* 9 and 12, hot chocolate 7 and 9, tea 10 and 12, wine 5.50 and 7, and beer 9.50 and 12 francs.

Near the funicular, the car that takes you up to Montmartre for the price of a métro ticket, is the **Restaurant Panoramique,** more a noisy souvenir stand with bar than anything else. Still, coffee is 6 and 12 francs, soda 15 and 20, beer 10 and 20, mineral water 15 and 20, and a sandwich 22 and 25. A few chairs and small tables outside give you a good view of the "lower town".

A la Mère Catherine is for those who want the Place du Tertre or nothing. Take the métro Anvers to the funicular, and follow the crowds to 6 Place du Tertre. Prices are relatively reasonable for the Place: coffee 16, hot chocolate 18, tea 16, beer 22 and 25, soda or wine 20.

A Cheapskate's Guide to Cafés

En Route

Useful cafés: if you're going to western France, to Angers or Nantes or somewhere else in the Loire Valley château country region—or simply coming in to Paris on the Air France bus—you may want to stop at Montparnasse. Across the street from the Montparnasse train station or *gare* is **L'Océan**, 43 avenue Maine, 75014 Paris (43.20.93.02). Métro: Montparnasse. L'Océan is a useful little café, open until 1 a.m. The reception is friendly and the prices—for being so near a major railway station—aren't bad. L'Océan has a glassed-in terrace. The decor could be described as Miami modern, recalling the late 1950s. There are coin telephones and the Air France bus from Orly stops right in front. We paid 10 francs for a coffee that would have cost 5 had we chosen to drink it at the bar; beer prices are 9 and 17, mineral water 7.50 and 16, and a sandwich 14 or 16 francs.

At the Charles de Gaulle/Roissy Airport, the **Bar du Point de Rencontre** in Terminal One, serving most flights to and from North America, is surprisingly reasonable. Here coffee is 5.70 francs, tea 14.50, beer 10.20, a croissant 6.50, juice 14.80, mineral water 12.70, coke 13.90, sandwiches 19 francs up, pie or *tarte* 17 francs, and pizza 24.30. The Bar du Point is near a newsstand and the board announcing arrivals, and right across from the tourist information office. Modern Deco style chairs and friendly service enhance the Point de Rencontre's appeal.

At Orly Sud, look for the small supermarket on the lower level where you can buy fruit, mineral water, French chocolate, and other treats to make your flight more tolerable. (I strongly recommend the large bottle of mineral water.) Right next to the supermarket is a simple little café, **Brioche Dorée**, part of a chain, where coffee is only 6 francs, a double 10. The Brioche is clean and pleasant.

For a better view, go up to the third floor to the **Bagatelle**

131

Café where you can sit facing an enormous window and watch planes taking off. Here coffee is still a reasonable 6.70 francs, a double *café crème* or espresso 13.40, a "special" espresso 9.30, beer 17, and a croissant 7.20. All are prices for travellers seated in the comfortable wicker chairs.

Flea Market

If you still have some time to spend in Paris, and you are a true cheapskate—I include myself, my friends, and most of my relatives in this category—you will eventually wind up at Les Puces, the real, the original flea market at Clignancourt. Take the métro to Clignancourt.

Two cafés were recommended by a knowledgeable-looking lady at a bookstore that sells original prints and lithographs, but it seemed to us that **Le Picolo** and **Le Péricole**, both on the rue Jules Vallès, do not have immediate charm: they may interest dealers as a place to meet and exchange gossip, but their generally grubby appearance and sometimes smart alecky waiters detract from their appeal. At Le Péricole, coffee is 5 francs and 7, beer 9 and 15, depending on where you consume it. Similar prices but no barstools are at Le Picolo, and the general look is plastic.

A relief from the typical flea market watering spots is **Le Saint Framboise**, 142 rue des Rosiers, 93400 Saint-Ouen (40.11.27.38). At Le Saint Framboise, coffee is 5 and 8 francs, tea, Coke, and beer 13 and 17. Don't be deterred by the stairs: on the rooftop terrace, you'd think the Puces were miles away— you're suddenly sitting at a beachside patio with yellow and white parasols over white tables. It's an oasis of peace.

12

Parisians Discuss Their Favorite Cafés

Cafés of Unusual Charm

"Right in the rue de Rivoli—it hasn't changed since Lenin used to come there, full of young people and of people of all kinds and all styles; where the old Marais and the Paris of passers-by cross, with very good wines, house cheese that's the strongest in Paris, the proprietress who's the worst tempered in Paris (in the world?), full of strayed yet happy tourists, open onto the street yet closed upon itself, noisy, familiar, enough room for people to sit down and a really long bar—that's already not bad."— Stephen, philosophy professor in Paris

This is **La Tartine** in the words of Stephen, who is French and a connoisseur of cafés in Paris. La Tartine is at 24 rue de Rivoli (42.72.76.85), and only a short walk—fifty meters—from the métro Saint-Paul. Coffee is 5.20 and 10 francs, beer

9.50 and 16, mineral water 13 and 17, and a sandwich 14 francs.

Attracted by his description, my husband and I went to La Tartine and found it to be everything a coffee drinker could wish for. This is old Paris at its best—charm and then some. The decor dates from the mid-nineteenth century, with burnt sienna and burgundy predominating, colors that have faded to just the right subtle shades. A variety of interesting sandwiches would make a low-priced lunch possible: ham, *saucisson*, pâté, and cheese, all on the special *pain poilâne*, are only 14 francs each, and a plate of cold cuts 40 francs. La Tartine is authentic and uncompromising, yet it seems strangely old, familiar, and comfortable: one would enjoy being a regular here.

On Sundays Christine, a young blonde Parisienne who works near the Tuileries, treats herself to something special: she goes to the **Deux Magots** for breakfast. She also likes to stop sometimes at the **Brasserie Lipp**, just across the street: "It's a nice setting—*très sympathique*. A good variety of people go there—foreigners, journalists, students—this is what makes good ambiance."

The Deux Magots and the Lipp are special—no doubt about that. But we observed many Parisians enjoying the historic setting of **Le Sélect**. Here, at 99 boulevard Montparnasse, is the only "American" café from the great days of the literary café to have kept its original interior. The light fixtures are pure Art Deco. If you want charm, history, atmosphere—this will be your place. Coffee 6 and 12 francs before 3:00 p.m., 10 and 15 after.

Stephen, who discovered La Tartine for us, also recommends the whole chain of **Ecluse** cafés, including:

L'Ecluse, 64 François 1er, 75008 Paris (47.20.77.09), near the Arc de Triomphe and the métro Georges V,

L'Ecluse Madeleine, 15 Place de la Madeleine, 75008 Paris (42.65.34.69), next to the famous restaurant Lucas Carton.

Marie, a Parisienne dancer specializing in Egyptian dance, likes cafés with impressive decor. Her favorites? Three café-bistrots in the 11th district: **Le Charbon**, at 109 rue Oberkampf, (43.57.55.13) from the Belle Epoque; **Les Couleurs**, 117 rue Saint-Maur, (43.57.95.61), which she says is "very popular with young people," and **Le Cannibale**, 93 rue Jean-Pierre Timbaud 75011 Paris (49.29.95.59). Also patronized by young Parisians, particularly at night, Le Cannibale has Second Empire decor. Service efficient and friendly. Coffee 5.5 and 9 francs.

Over in the 20th arrondissement, near the Père Lachaise cemetery, final resting place for Oscar Wilde, Abelard and Heloise, Jim Morrison, and a host of others, is **Le Saint Amour**, at 32 boulevard Ménilmontant (47.97.20.15). (This neighborhood is where Edith Piaf was born, and where "the little sparrow" started out by singing on the streets.) A wine bar, brasserie, restaurant, and tearoom, Le Saint Amour specializes in products from Auvergne served with the famous *poilâne* bread. It is open from 11:30 a.m. to 10 p.m.—on Sunday until 8:30—and closed on Mondays. "One of the best," remarks Stephen.

"La Route des Zincs," an article in *Figaroscope* magazine, identified three cafés as outstanding for their ambiance and charm. **Le Brin de Zinc . . . et Madame**, at 50 rue Montorgueil, 75002 Paris (42.21.10.80), has a superb, authentic bar dating from the turn of the century. The good traditional cuisine includes daily specials. The second recommendation, **Le Temps des Cerises**, at 31 rue de la Cerisaie, 75004 Paris (42.21.10.80), is one of our own old favorites, already described in "Maigret's Cafés," and "Country Cafés" (see pp. 39 & 97). A third, **Le Brissemoret**, at 5 rue Saint-Marc, 75002 Paris (42.36.91.72), originally had a bar made of pewter. It was replaced by the more conventional zinc after the war. The proprietor, who is described as having a "*rétro*" soul, cooks up dishes worth savoring.

The Cafés of Paris

Neighborhood Cafés

A young Parisienne, Masha, likes a café in the 11th arrondissement: **Le Rey**, 1 rue du Faubourg Saint-Antoine, 75011 Paris (43.43.19.30). Here she can have coffee for 5 and 8 francs, beer or wine for 10. What is special about Le Rey? "This café is frequented by friends, it's a place to get together on Saturday nights before going to eat at a restaurant, for example. We like to celebrate the 'beaujolais nouveau' there." Masha knows the proprietor and the barmen—she adds that it's a café "kept by people from the Auvergne, who organize soirées with someone playing the accordion, playing old French folksongs."

She doesn't care much for some of the more celebrated cafés like **Les Deux Magots** or **Le Père Tranquille**, and goes on to explain why. In her opinion, the famous cafés tend to be

elitist, reserved for tourists or fashionable French people, because the prices at these cafés are really out of reach, as well as for those cafés in certain areas–the Champs-Elysées, the old Opéra, and recently the Bastille Opéra. For coffee on the terrasse you have to figure on 15 or 20 francs.

Little French cafés are frequented by people who work or live nearby. Certain people eat lunch in the same café for years or go to have a before-dinner drink to relax in the evening. A café in France is a place to meet people where you talk about everything and nothing (although at the bar they talk mostly politics). . . . People who drink one espresso coffee do it to give themselves a "jolt," usually passing through after resting in the afternoon, or else you have arranged to meet someone, then you wait for them while drinking one cup of coffee because it's the least expensive drink.

Terry is a young French architect who not only worked on EuroDisney, but has several impressive buildings to his credit in the Pantin district. He singles out **Le Bouquet** at 25 rue

136

Daguerre, 75014 Paris (43.22.54.19), as a café worth a stop. Coffee is 4.80 and 7 francs, beer 9 and 14, and wine 5.60 and 7.60 francs. "It's a homey café with a clientele of regulars, in a simple decor, with the wood bar still covered with zinc," he says. The habitués tend to be "intellectuals, businessmen from the district, executives, employees, and workers. Very few students—they prefer a different ambiance." The clientele of Le Bouquet includes actors Jean-Paul Belmondo and Jean Claude Dreyffus.

His favorite café? "In my opinion, the café that seems the most pleasant is **Chez Peret** on the rue Daguerre." Why? "A wine bar, with an excellent cellar, and main room small enough for people to talk and get to know each other."

Michèle, a blonde social worker, likes to drop in at **Le Saint Sébastien**, 42 rue Saint-Sébastien, 75011 Paris (48.06.48.05). Here coffee is 4.80 and 5.50 francs, and a beer 6 francs at the bar. She enjoys the ambiance: "It's an old café without any particular decoration, in the style of the '70s, not really very attractive to look at but the customers are nice and the atmosphere friendly—the clientele are local people from this district."

Like Terry, Michèle also recommends **Chez Peret**, at 6 rue Daguerre in the 14th arrondissement (43.22.57.05), which she considers an old-style bistro: "They serve very good Burgundy and Beaujolais wines, and sandwiches made with good regional ingredients—good breads, cheeses, and meats of a very high quality."

Alexandra, a university student living in the 14th arrondissement, casts another vote for Chez Peret: "Everybody in my building goes there," she says, adding that *café au lait* will cost 16 or 18 francs.

Katherine and Charles, professors with an apartment in the 15th arrondissement, sometimes go across Paris to the Place de la République during the winter. There they visit **Le Thermomètre**, at 4 Place de la République, 75011 Paris (47.00.30.78). Métro: République. Katherine describes how appealing the warm, glassed-in *terrasse* can be—a place to sit and feel cozy, with a good view of passers-by and the Place when the weather outside is cold and damp. She says that the *toilettes* are particularly worth a visit—marble and gold luxury! At Le Thermomètre, coffee is 13 francs, hot chocolate 19, tea 21, beer 21 francs and up, and wine 23 francs and up.

Charles favors **Le Marigny,** at 108 rue de la Convention, 75015 Paris (45.54.64.40), because of its superb *salade niçoise.* He considers it the best in France, "far better than any poor thing they now make in Nice or in the run of establishments in Paris." Katherine usually orders one of their good omelettes, available for around 25 to 27 francs.

Cafés with Great Locations

Imke and Alexandra, university students living in central Paris, rave about the **Café de la Mairie,** 8 Place Saint-Sulpice, 75006 Paris (43.26.67.82), where the location is particularly appealing. Alexandra has found it possible to get to know some of the regulars. She likes the varied clientele: "All sorts of people go there and one can sit outside—the church [Saint-Sulpice] is very pretty."

Another café recommended by a local resident is **Le Mistral,** at 2 Place du Châtelet (42.78.13.99). Métro: Châtelet. From Le Mistral, you have splendid views of Notre Dame, the Conciergerie and part of the Eiffel Tower. A Parisienne with a shop on the rue de Rivoli told us it's her children's favorite café. At Le Mistral, coffee is 5.20 and 11 francs, beer 9.50 and 18, soda or juice 15 and 20, mineral water 13 and 18, and a sandwich 15 and 17 francs.

Dominique sells authentic Art Nouveau and Art Deco posters from a shop in the 6th district. She likes **Le Racine** at 3 rue Racine, in the 6th district, **Le Bistrot du Peintre,** 116 avenue Ledru-Rollin 11th district and, for especially good ambiance and great service, **Le Pause Café,** 41 rue de Charonne.

"The café I like is the one in the Jardin," said a boutique owner who has an unusual gift shop near the Jardin du Luxembourg, specializing in items including gift wrap, writing paper, and knickknacks all relating to music. She loves to go to the **Café Goufre** right in front of the Senate in the Jardin du Luxembourg. In the winter it's so quiet and tranquil there that she imagines herself in some remote part of Canada. This café is more fully described in "Country Cafés and Salons de Thé." If you want an escape from the polluted air and noise of busy streets in the touristy 6th district, this is the café for you.

One question I like to ask Parisians is where they would direct a person visiting the city for the first time. Françoise Cachin, curator of the Musée d'Orsay, was interviewed by *Paris le Journal*. When asked much the same question, she remarked: "When I have friends coming to Paris for the first time, I get them to go to the *terrasse* of the Samaritaine, a café which is beyond price." The **Samaritaine Café**, situated on the roof of the Samaritaine department store, offers one of the finest views of the city. It's a view that can be appreciated by anyone with 10 francs for a cup of coffee.

Students' Cafés

"Students often meet in the café which is closest to their school, drinking only one cup of coffee and staying there for hours to talk and work, because they don't have much money."—Masha

Stéphanie, a tall, attractive university student now living in the suburbs, told us about **Le Rendez-vous des Belges**, at 23 rue Dunkerque, 75010 Paris (42.82.04.72), in front of the **Gare du Nord**. Métro: Gare du Nord. This is a café she drops into perhaps twice a week. Coffee is 7 or 8 francs there, she tells us, *café au lait* 11 francs, and beer 20 francs (all prices for customers who are seated). She describes the clientele as being mostly people who are on their way somewhere, so "it's the presence of students that gives the place ambiance. And the staff are friendly."

Jérôme, a student from Neuilly, considers **Le Flore**, at 172 boulevard Saint-Germain, 75006 Paris (45.48.55.26), the best café in Paris, because "it's famous and the ambiance is very nice—coffee 35 francs a cup." (Actually he has an exaggerated notion of the current prices—coffee in the historic setting of Le Flore is still available for 21 francs.)

Christophe is engrossed in his studies of advanced physics, yet finds time to drop into a café. His favorite is **El Amigo**, at 59 rue des Archives, 75003 Paris (40.29.02.97). Here an espresso is 4.80 francs. The café is well named, because when asked about its specific characteristics, Christophe emphasizes the friendliness of the place—he's already met people there and has come to know the proprietor and the barmen—something not always easy to do in a large city.

Another student, Imke, a long-time resident of Paris and a talented violinist, favors **Au Bistrot de la Sorbonne**, at 4 rue Touiller, 75005 Paris (40.33.41.49), métro Luxembourg or Saint-Michel, and **Le Vavin**, at 18 rue Vavin, 75006 Paris (43.26.67.47), near the Alliance Française, métro Odéon. She says that coffee is about 8 francs at the bar, 10 if you're seated, and a small glass of wine from 10 francs up. At La Sorbonne, she appreciates the lively ambiance created by the students who are regulars there. Le Vavin she finds more chic but still appealing, although she adds, "It's not the sort of place you go to every day."

A vivacious and attractive professor of French, Géva, lives in the 17th arrondissement, near the Place de Clichy, but recommends **Doucet**, at 25 rue d'Assas, 75006 Paris, near the Institut Catholique. Here coffee is 5.50 and 9 francs, and a glass of wine—which she says is by no means *ordinaire*—from 8 francs. At Doucet, she observes "a lively, joyful, and very Parisian mixture of people, including students and working-class people at the same time. It's crowded at certain periods—around 11 a.m. and at mealtimes—and quieter before and after."

Famous Cafés

Asked about historic cafés, several Parisians singled out the **Café Le Croissant** as a place where history was made when Jean Jaurès, who had opposed France's entry into World War I, was assassinated in the café on the eve of hostilities. A marble plaque outside commemorates this historic event. But even for people who are not interested in its history, Le Croissant is worth a visit. Situated at 146 rue Montmartre (42.33.35.04), near the métro Bourse, Le Croissant has attractive wood panelling, an oak bar, and pink granite instead of the usual grey marble in the classic small round tables. Here coffee is 5.50 and 8.50 francs, fruit juice 14 and 17, beer 9.50 and 14, and a sandwich 14 and 17.

If you happen to be in the 6th arrondissement, Stephen suggests you try the **Procope**, the oldest café in Paris, at 13 rue de l'Ancienne Comédie, 75006 Paris (43.26.99.20). Métro: Odéon. He adds that although it is mainly a restaurant, there is still part of the Procope that remains a café-bar. So you can have coffee where Benjamin Franklin and the leaders of the French Revolution used to dine.

Two friendly librarians in the reserve section of the **Musée Pompidou**, or **Beaubourg**, recommended the **Café Beaubourg** at 43 rue Saint-Merri, 75004 Paris (48.87.63.96), facing the museum. Métro: Rambuteau. Their information on prices was a little vague: "You should be able to get out of there for 10 francs," one said. Actually, a basic espresso costs 16 francs, or 18 after 7 p.m., but the ambiance makes up for it.

Perhaps the two of the most famous cafés in Paris are the **Deux Magots** and the **Café Flore**. (The Lipp, opposite, is a *brasserie*). Oscar Wilde would stop in at the Deux Magots after he left England, and James Joyce went there for white wine. Now with fashionable French people the Flore is "in," and the Deux Magots "out." As a Frenchman explained to Adam Gopnik of the *New Yorker*, "If you place any two things side by side, one will become fashionable and the other will not. It's a necessity determined by the nature of fashion."

Afflicted with a *trou de mémoire*—a memory lapse—one Parisian could not recall a specific name for his favorite café, but said one could find good cafés by going to the Place des Vosges and taking the *passage* near the house of Victor Hugo. Following his advice, we found ourselves at **L'Olivier**, 6 rue de Birague, 75004 Paris (42.72.90.38). Métro: Bastille or Saint-Paul. L'Olivier is a charming little restaurant in a quiet street a few yards from the Place des Vosges. We were right next to a café with an intriguing old-style façade—**Le Vieux Comptoir**, 8 rue Birague, 75004 Paris (42.72.17.80), unfortunately closed in August.

The Café in Parisians' Lives

Several people I spoke with shared their feeling that the local café is more than just a place of business: that it touches their lives in important ways. Marie Louise, a teacher who lives near the République, often stops at **Au Béranger** on Saturday mornings after she and her friends have done their shopping at the market. Au Béranger is an attractive café at 180 rue du Temple, 75003 Paris (42.72.72.45). Here the proprietor has even given her and her friends their cups of coffee "on the house," a generous and unusual gesture in a city the size of Paris. Terry, who lives in the same area, cited the warmth and friendliness of people who run the café at the street level: "They ask about us—we ask about them. We find out what's going on and how everyone is. It can be just like a village here."

Géva, a professor at the Institut Catholique, likes to stop at **Au Sauvignon**, 80 rue des Saints-Pères, 75007 Paris (45.48.49.02), near the métro Sèvres-Babylone, because, as she says, "you can drink good wines there and eat delicious sandwiches, and the café is always full. You can sit down, but the ambiance is very *sympa*—friendly—when you stand at the bar." Au Sauvignon is closed on Sundays, in August, and during the school break in February.

In *Le Quotidien de Paris*, Geneviève Huttin, formerly a professor of philosophy and now a writer, spoke about what the Parisian cafés mean to her. Asked about the difference between cafés in the country and those in Paris, Huttin noted that cafés in eastern France, where she used to live, are "first of all a man's world where men meet each other there at specific times to have discussions. For me at that time the café was only a refuge, a place to spend time. I wasn't integrated into local society, so, when one doesn't have a place of one's own, there's nothing left but the café. When I came to Paris, what impressed me was the diversity and multiplicity of cafés. I love to hear other languages, other sounds, to discover the traces of another culture than our own. The Café de la Mosquée in Paris is an astonishing place for that reason."

The **Café de la Mosquée** is at 39 rue Geoffroy-Saint-Hilaire, 75005 Paris (43.31.18.14). Métro: Jussieu or Monge. Open daily except in August, from 11 a.m. to 9 p.m., the café gives one the feeling of the mosque itself, with its Moorish-influenced interior.

To Huttin, the appeal of a Parisian café has to do with the ready acceptance she has always found there:

Cafés are the only places where I can push a door open, enter, sit down at a table without asking anyone for anything and without anyone paying attention to me. There I feel completely free. The café is a place where one can completely

143

forget the social role one plays in everyday life. You have people around you, but surprisingly, you find a sort of anonymity, a peacefulness that suits me.

It is my hope that you will come to find your own special café where you can experience the true Paris and enjoy the warmth of the City of Light. As Joseph Barry put it, "Ever since there have been Americans, they have dreamed a dream and called it Paris." May this book bring you a little closer to realizing your dream.

Cafés by Location and Price of Coffee

Name	Arr.	Address	Telephone	Price(F)		Page
				bar	table	
Angelina	75001	226 rue de Rivoli	42.60.82.00	na	20	p. 106
Bar du Caveau	75001	17 Pl. Dauphine	43.54.45.95	na	12	p. 49
Béarn, Le	75001	2 Pl. St.-Opportune	42.36.93.35	5	8	p. 47
Café Samaritaine	75001	19 rue de la Monnaie	40.41.20.20	na	10	p. 124
Castiglione, Le	75001	235 rue St.-Honoré	42.60.68.22	6	13	p. 58
Cochon à l'Oreille	75001	15 rue Montmartre	42.36.07.56	5.50	8	p. 96
Coupe d'Or, La	75001	330 rue St.-Honoré	42.60.43.26	6.50	12	p. 59
Cour Couronné, Au	75001	6 rue Ferronnerie	45.08.11.15	na	10	p. 25
Dauphin, Le	75001	167 rue St.-Honoré	42.60.40.11	6	10	p. 59
Dogs Café	75001	7 rue Cossonnerie	42.21.37.24	na	12	p. 85
Front Page, Le	75001	58 rue St.-Denis	42.36.98.69	na	10	p. 86
Lina's Sandwiches	75001	4 rue Cambon	40.15.94.95	6	6	p. 59
Marly, Le Café	75001	93 rue de Rivoli	49.26.06.60	16	16	p. 96
Petit Voisin, Le now L'Agenterie	75001	5 rue Cambon	42.60.10.34	5.50	11	p. 59
Piccadilly Tearoom	75001	10 rue Cambon	42.60.14.12	5.50	5.50	p. 59
Samaritaine, Terrasse de,	75001	19 rue de la Monnaie	43.33.96.70	na	10	p. 124
Tavern, Guinness	75001	31 rue des Lombards	42.33.26.45	5	10	p. 38
Taverne Henri IV	75001	13 Pl. Pont Neuf	43.54.27.90	6	na	p. 49
Ver Luisant, Au	75001	26 rue Mont Thabor	42.60.83.69	5.50	8	p. 59
Vieux Chatelet, Au	75001	1 Place du Chatelet	42.33.79.27	5.80	12	p. 60
Zimmer, Le	75001	1 Pl. du Châtelet	42.38.74.03	na	13	p. 60

na = not available

Name	Arr.	Address	Telephone	Price(F) bar	Price(F) table	Page
A Priori Thé	75002	35 Galerie Vivienne	42.97.48.75	na	12	p. 106
Aiglon, L'	75002	12 rue Vivienne	42.60.08.83	5	7	p. 70
Bar Louis le Grand	75002	1 rue Louis le Grand	40.15.09.58	5.70	10	p. 59
Brazza, Le	75002	86 rue Montmartre	na	5.20	8.50	p. 38
Brin de Zinc..Et Mme	75002	50 rue Montorgueil	42.21.10.80	na	na	p. 135
Brissemoret	75002	5 rue St.-Marc	42.36.91.72	na	na	p. 135
Café du Croissant	75002	146 rue Montmartre	42.33.35.04	5.50	8.50	p. 141
Colombe, La	75002	2 rue de la Paix	42.61.09.69	6	12	p. 58
Dauphin Bleu, Le	75002	rue St.-Denis/ E. Marcel	42.21.98.40	5	9	p. 85
Grain de Café, Le	75002	4 Pl. de l'Opéra	42.66.99.78	5.70	11	p. 71
Paris-Montmartre, Le	75002	106 rue Montmartre	42.33.17.13	5	8	p. 38
Tambour, Le	75002	41 rue Montmartre	42.33.06.90	5.50	8	p. 38
Thé au Fil	75002	1 rue Chaptal	42.36.95.49	na	11	p. 107
Vaudeville, Le	75002	29 rue Vivienne	40.20.04.62	5.50	8	p. 70
Bar 14	75003	14 rue de Bretagne	40.72.20.66	4.50	6.50	p. 121
Béranger, Au	75003	180 rue du Temple	42.72.72.45	6	12	p. 142
Brocco	75003	178 rue du Temple	42.72.19.81	na	8.50	p. 107
Café des Musées	75003	49 rue de Turenne	42.72.96.17	6.50	11.50	p. 46
Marais Plus, Le	75003	20 rue Francs-Bourgeois	48.87.01.40	na	10	p. 105
Taverne, Bar Belge	75003	5 Pl. de la République	42.78.50.86	7	12.50	p. 129
Barcane L'Oulette	75004	38 rue des Tournelles	42.71.43.33	—	—	p. 47
Boulangerie-Caf.	75004	149 rue St.-Martin	42.72.64.60	7.50	7.50	p. 125
Bourgogne, Ma	75004	19 Place des Vosges	42.78.44.64	6	14	p. 46

na = not available

146

Name	Arr.	Address	Telephone	Price(F) bar	Price(F) table	Page
Bugat, Paul	75004	5 bd. Beaumarchais	48.87.89.88	na	12	p. 107
Café Beaubourg	75004	43 rue St-Merri	48.87.63.96	na	16	p. 141
Cavalier Bleu, Le	75004	rue Rambuteau/St-Martin	na	5.80	10	p. 125
Comédie, La	75004	11 rue de la Reynie	42.71.22.29	6	9	p. 96
Deux Palais, Les	75004	3 bd. du Palais	43.54.20.86	6	12.50	p. 49
Drapeau, Au (Flag Café)	75004	3 bd. Beaumarchais	42.72.05.28	5.50	9	p. 45
Enfants Gâtés, Les	75004	43 rue Francs-Bourgeois	42.77.07.63	na	15	p. 47
Gamin de Paris, Au	75004	51 rue Vieille du Temple	42.78.97.24	5.50	11	p. 123
Locandiera Bar	75004	27 rue de Turenne	40.27.93.10	6	8	p. 123
Lutetia, Le	75004	33 quai de Bourbon	43.54.11.71	6	11	p. 125
Lys d'Argent, Au	75004	90 rue St-Louis en l'île	46.33.56.13	na	10	p. 125
Martini, Café	75004	11 rue Pas de Mule	42.77.05.04	6	10	p. 123
Mont Lozère	75004	131 rue Saint-Martin	48.87.73.00	9	12	p. 96
Olivier, L' (resto)	75004	6 rue Birague	42.71.90.38	5	8	p. 142
Paris-Midi	75004	2 Quai de Gesves	42.72.00.04	5	10	p. 123
Perla, La	75004	26 rue François Miron	42.77.59.40	6	12	p. 48
Petit Fer à Cheval	75004	30 rue Vieille du Temple	42.72.47.47	11	15	p. 95
Quasimodo N.-D.	75004	11 rue d'Arcole	43.54.19.45	5.80	10	p. 124
Saint Régis, Le	75004	6 rue Jean du Bellay	43.54.59.41	6	11.50	p. 124
Tartine, La	75004	24 rue de Rivoli	42.72.76.85	5.20	10	p. 133
Temps des Cerises, Le	75004	31 rue de la Cerisaie	42.72.08.63	6.70	9.50	p. 104
Vieux Comptoir, Le	75004	8 rue Birague	42.72.17.80	6	10	p. 142
Bistrot de la Sorbonne	75005	4 rue Touiller	40.33.41.49	8	10	p. 140
Départ, Au	75005	1 rue Gay-Lussac	46.34.63.98	5.50	10	p. 126

na = not available

147

Name	Arr.	Address	Telephone	Price(F) bar	Price(F) table	Page
Mosquée, Café de la	75005	39 rue Geoffrey-St.-Hilaire	43.31.18.14	na	na	p. 143
Bar de l'Institut	75006	21 rue de Seine	43.26.98.75	5.50	7	p. 127
Boul' Mich, Le	75006	116 bd. St.-Germain	46.33.76.66	5.50	11	p. 15
Brasserie L'Atlas	75006	11 rue de Buci	43.25.43.94	5	10	p. 57
Brasserie Lipp	75006	151 bd. St.-Germain	45.48.53.91	18	18	p. 13
Calumet, Le	75006	30 N.-D.-des-Champs	na	5	10	p. 14
Christine, Le	75006	1 rue Christine	40.51.71.64	6	12	p. 37
Closerie des Lilas	75006	171 bd. Montparnasse	43.26.70.50	na	18	p. 12
Danton, Le	75006	103 bd. St.-Germain	43.54.65.38	5.70	11	p. 15
Deux Magots, Les	75006	6 Pl. St.-Germain	45.48.55.25	na	22	p. 13
Doucet	75006	25 rue d'Assas	na	5.50	9	p. 140
Ecluse, L'	75006	15 quai Grands-Augustins	46.33.58.74	na	na	p. 57
Flore, Le	75006	172 bd. St.-Germain	45.48.55.26	na	21	p. 35
Goufre, Café	75006	Jdn du Luxembourg	na	na	9	p. 104
Latin Odéon	75006	126 bd. St.-Germain	43.26.92.24	na	12	p. 58
Lina's Sandwiches	75006	27 rue St.-Sulpice	43.29.14.14	6	6	p. 119
Mairie, Café de la	75006	8 Pl. St.-Sulpice	43.26.67.82	5.60	11.50	p. 37
Mazet, Le	75006	61 rue St.-André	43.54.68.81	5.50	10	p. 58
Palette, La	75006	43 rue de Seine	43.26.68.15	6	12	p. 97
Pré aux Clercs, Le	75006	30 rue Bonaparte	43.54.41.73	6	13	p. 15
Procope, Le	75006	13 rue l'Ancienne Comédie	43.26.99.20	na	15	p. 24
Relais Odéon	75006	132 bd. St.-Germain	43.29.81.80	5.50	12	p. 24
Rhumerie, La	75006	166 bd. St.-Germain	43.54.28.94	na	12	p. 57
Rotonde, La	75006	105 bd. du Montparnasse	43.26.68.84	12	15	p. 14

na = not available

Name	Arr.	Address	Telephone	Price(F) bar	Price(F) table	Page
Saint-André, Le	75006	2 rue Danton	43.26.56.59	5.50	11.50	p. 15
Sélect, Le	75006	99 bd. du Montparnasse	45.48.38.24	6.10	15	p. 95
Tournon, Le	75006	18 rue de Tournon	na	5.50	10	p. 15
Trait d'Union	75006	122 rue de Rennes	45.48.70.66	5.50	10.50	p. 15
Vieux Colombier, Au	75006	65 rue de Rennes	45.48.53.81	5.60	12	p. 14
Bar du Pont Royal	75007	7 rue Montalembert	45.44.38.27	na	na	p. 38
Côté Jardin	75007	22 rue de Sèvres	44.39.80.00	15	15	p. 107
Relais de la Tour	75007	27 ave. la Bourdonnais	47.05.44.93	6	11	p. 127
Royal Tour	75007	23 ave. la Bourdonnais	47.05.04.54	6	11	p. 128
Sauvignon, Au	75007	80 rue de Saints-Pères	45.48.49.02	na	na	p. 143
Voltaire, Le	75007	27 quai Voltaire	42.61.17.49	5	10	p. 26
Café Madeleine	75008	35 Pl. Madeleine	42.65.21.91	6	13	p. 69
Fauchon	75008	30 Pl. Madeleine	47.42.60.11	6.80	6.80	p. 120
Francis, Chez	75008	7 Pl. de l'Alma	47.23.39.53	20	20	p. 128
Fouquet's	75008	99 ave. Champs-Elysées	47.23.70.60	na	25	p. 37
Ladurée	75008	16 rue Royale	42.60.21.79	na	18	p. 70
Lanvin Espace Café Bleu	75008	15 rue du Fbg. St-Honoré	44.71.32.32	5	18	p. 68
Paris London, Le	75008	16 Pl. Madeleine	47.42.33.92	5.50	11	p. 69
Peny, Le	75008	3 Pl. Madeleine	42.65.06.75	6.50	14	p. 105
Théâtres, Bar des	75008	6 ave. Montaigne	47.23.34.63	10	15	p. 68
Batifol	75009	3 Pl. Blanche	48.74.39.37	8	12	p. 128
Chiba	75009	28 rue Vignon	47.42.01.24	9	9	p. 108

na = not available

149

Name	Arr.	Address	Telephone	Price(F) bar	Price(F) table	Page
Entr'acte, L'	75009	1 rue Auber	47.42.26.25	5.80	13	p. 68
Grain de Café, Le	75009	4 Pl. de l'Opera	42.66.99.78	6	na	p. 71
Paix, Café de la	75009	12 bd. Capucines	42.68.12.13	na	26	p. 68
Sans-Souci, Le	75009	65 rue Pigalle	48.74.37.28	5	10	p. 85
Bistrot du Peintre	75011	116 ave. Ledru-Rollin	47.00.34.39	6	10	p. 122
Café Le Bastille	75011	8 Pl. de la Bastille	43.07.79.95	6	14	p. 122
Café Le Paris	75011	24 bd. Richard-Lenoir	47.00.87.47	5.50	10	p. 45
Cannibale, Le	75011	93 rue J. P. Timbaud	49.29.95.59	5.50	9	p. 135
Clown Bar, Le	75011	114 rue Amelot	43.55.87.35	10	12	p. 45
Industrie, Café de L'	75011	16 rue St.-Sabin	47.00.13.53	5.50	9	p. 46
Pause Café, Le	75011	41 rue de Charonne	48.06.80.33	5.80	10	p. 122
Relais d'Eguisheim, Le	75011	6 Pl. de la République	47.00.44.10	na	13	p. 42
Rey, Le	75011	1 rue Fbg. St.-Antoine	43.43.19.30	5	8	p. 136
Thermomètre, Le	75011	4 Pl. de la République	47.00.30.78	na	13	p. 42
Merle Moqueur, Le	75013	11 Butte aux Cailles	45.65.12.43	na	na	p. 86
Bouquet, Le	75014	25 rue Daguerre	43.22.54.19	na	na	p. 137
Coupole, La	75014	102 bd. du Montparnasse	43.20.14.20	6	12	p. 12
Dôme, Le	75014	108 bd. du Montparnasse	43.35.25.81	8	15	p. 35
Océan, L'	75014	43 ave. Maine	43.20.93.02	5	10	p. 131
Peret, Antoine	75014	6 rue Daguerre	43.22.57.05	16	18	p. 137
Marigny, Le	75015	108 rue la Convention	45.54.64.40	5	8	p. 138

na = not available

150

Cafés by Location and Price of Coffee

Name	Arr.	Address	Telephone	Price(F) bar	Price(F) table	Page
Flandrin, Le	75016	80 ave. Henri-Martin	45.04.34.69	7.50	15	na
Balto, Le	75018	58 rue Custine	46.06.17.88	5.50	10	p. 129
Bohème du Tertre	75018	2 Pl. du Tertre	46.06.51.69	20	24	p. 75
Carrousel, Le	75018	8 rue des 3 Frères	42.23.82.62	na	9	p. 75
Clairon des Chasseurs	75018	3 Pl. du Tertre	42.62.40.08	6	12	p. 76
Crêpe à Pic, La	75018	35 rue Lepic	42.55.95.95	na	9	p. 130
Gavroche, Le	75018	22 rue Hermel	46.06.40.63	5	8	p. 130
Lapin Agile, Le	75018	22 rue des Saules	46.06.85.87	na	90	p. 92
Mère Catherine, A La	75018	6 Pl. du Tertre	46.06.32.69	10	18	p. 75
Négociants, Aux	75018	27 rue Lambert	46.06.15.11	5.50	9	p. 75
Nord-Sud, Le	75018	79 rue Mont Cenis	46.06.02.87	5.50	11	p. 75
Relais, Au	75018	48 rue Lamarck	46.06.68.32	6	10	p. 75
Sancerre, Le	75018	35 rue de Abbesses	42.58.08.20	na	na	p. 92
Tabac des Deux Moulins	75018	15 rue Lepic	42.54.90.50	na	na	p. 85
Tabac de la Mairie	75018	28 rue Hermel	46.06.01.30	5.50	10.50	p. 92
Saint Amour, Le	75020	32 bd. Ménilmontant	47.97.20.15	na	na	p. 135
Bagatelle Café	Orly	Orly Sud Airport	na	6.70	6.70	p. 132
Point de Rencontre	Roissy	Charles de Gaulle Airport	na	6	7	p. 131
Saint Framboise	St. Ouen	142 rue des Rosiers	42.11.27.38	7	9	p. 132

na = not available

Cafés by Nearest Attraction

Attraction	Café	Address	Métro	Page
Arc de Triomphe	Drugstore, Le	133 ave. Champs-Elysées	Georges-V	*
Arc de Triomphe	Fouquet's	99 ave. Champs-Elysées	Georges-V	p. 36
Bastille	Café Le Bastille	8 Pl. de la Bastille	Bastille	p. 122
Bastille	Caoua	207 rue Fbg-St.-Antoine	Faidherbe	*
Bastille	Caves St. Gilles	4 rue St.-Gilles	Bastille	*
Bastille	Gamin de Paris, Au	51 rue Vieille du Temple	St.-Paul	p. 46
Bastille	Industrie, Café de L'	16 rue St.-Sabin	Bastille	p. 46
Bastille	Peintre, Bistrot du	116 ave Ledru-Rollin	Bastille	p. 122
Bastille	Rey, Le	1 rue Fbg-St.-Antoine	Bastille	p. 136
Bastille	Temps des Cerises, Le	31 rue de la Cerisaie	Bastille	p. 104
Bibliothèque Nationale	Coq Hardi, Au	9 rue Paul Lelong	Sentier	*
Bourse	A Priori Thé	35 Galerie Vivienne	Bourse	p. 106
Bourse	Aiglon, L'	12 rue Vivienne	Bourse	p. 70
Bourse	Brissemoret	5 rue St.-Marc	Rue Montmartre	p. 135
Bourse	Vaudeville, Le	29 rue Vivienne	Bourse	p. 70
Catacombs	Peret, Antoine	6 rue Daguerre	Denfert-Roch.	p. 137
Centre Pompidou	Boulangerie-Caf.	149 rue St.-Martin	Rambuteau	p. 125
Centre Pompidou	Café Beaubourg	100 rue St.-Martin	Rambuteau	p. 141
Centre Pompidou	Cavalier Bleu, Le	rue Rambuteau/St.-Martin	Rambuteau	p. 125
Centre Pompidou	Comédie, La	11 rue de la Regnie	Rambuteau	p. 125

* Not mentioned in the text, but convenient to the attraction

Attraction	Café	Address	Métro	Page
Centre Pompidou	Mont Lozère	131 rue St.-Martin	Rambuteau	p. 96
Centre Pompidou	Tavern, Guinness	31 rue des Lombards	Châtelet	p. 37
Ch. de Gaulle Airport	Point de Rencontre, Bar du	Ch. de Gaulle Airport	RER Roissy	p. 131
Cirque d'Hiver	Clown Bar, Le	114 rue Amelot	Filles-du-Calvaire	p. 45
Cluny Museum	Boul' Mich, Le	116 bd. St.-Germain	St.-Michel	p. 15
Cluny Museum	Saint André, Le	2 rue Danton	St.-Michel	p. 15
Conciergerie	Taverne Henri IV	13 Pl. Pont Neuf	Pont-Neuf	p. 49
Eiffel Tower	Chez Francis	7 Pl. de l'Alma	Alma-Marceau	p. 128
Eiffel Tower	Relais de la Tour	27 ave. La Bourdonnais	Champs de Mars	p. 127
Eiffel Tower	Royal Tour	23 ave. La Bourdonnais	Champs de Mars	p. 128
Eiffel Tower	Tabac de l'Alma	5 ave. Rapp	Champs de Mars	*
Flea Market	St. Framboise, Le	142 rue des Rosiers	Clignancourt	p. 132
Fontaine Innocents	Cour Couronné, Au	6 rue Ferronnerie	Châtelet	p. 25
Forum des Halles	Brazza, Le	86 rue Montmartre	Sentier	p. 38
Forum des Halles	Brin de Zinc..Et Mme	50 rue Montorgueil	Les Halles	p. 135
Forum des Halles	Dogs Café	7 rue Cossonnerie	Châtelet	p. 85
Forum des Halles	Front Page, Le	58 rue St.-Denis	Châtelet	p. 86
Forum des Halles	Paris-Montmartre, Le	106 rue Montmartre	Châtelet	p. 38

* Not mentioned in the text, but convenient to the attraction

Attraction	Café	Address	Métro	Page
Forum des Halles	Père Tranquille, Au	16 rue Pierre Lescot	Chatelet	p. 136
Forum des Halles	Dauphin Bleu, Le	rue St.-Denis/ E. Marcel	Etienne Marcel	p. 85
Grand Palais	Théâtres, Bar des	6 ave. Montaigne	Alma-Marceau	p. 68
Hôtel de Ville	Café Samaritaine	19 rue de la Monnaie	Pont Neuf/Châtelet	p. 26
Hôtel de Ville	Béarn, Le	2 Pl. St.-Opportune	Châtelet	p. 46
Hôtel de Ville	Bouchon du Marais, Au	15 rue François Miron	Hôtel de Ville	p. 123
Hôtel de Ville	Paris-Midi	2 quai de Gesves	Hôtel de Ville	p. 48
Hôtel de Ville	Perla, La	26 rue François Miron	Hôtel de Ville	p. 133
Hôtel de Ville	Tartine, La	24 rue de Rivoli	St. Paul	
Ile Saint Louis	Lys d'Argent, Au	rue St. L. en île/Brtd	Pont Marie	p. 125
Ile Saint Louis	Saint Régis, Le	6 rue Jean du Bellay	Pont Marie	p. 124
Ile Saint Louis	Lutetia, Le	33 quai de Bourbon	Pont Marie	p. 125
Institut de France	Bar de l'Institut	21 rue de Seine	St.-Germain	p. 127
Jardin du Luxembourg	Départ, Au	1 rue Gay-Lussac	Luxembourg	p. 126
Jardin du Luxembourg	Christine, Le	1 rue Christine	Odéon	p. 37
Jardin du Luxembourg	Trait d'Union	122 rue de Rennes	St. Placide	p. 15
Jardin du Luxembourg	Goutre, Café	Jdn du Luxembg	Luxembourg	p. 104
Louvre	Marly, Le Café	93 rue de Rivoli	Palais-Royal	p. 96
Louvre	Coupe d'Or, La	330 rue St.-Honoré	Tuileries	p. 59
Louvre	Voltaire, Le	27 quai Voltaire	Rue du Bac	p. 26
Louvre	Angelina	226 rue de Rivoli	Concorde	p. 106
Louvre	Petit Voisin, Le	5 rue Cambon	Concorde	p. 59

154

Attraction	Café	Address	Métro	Page
Madeleine	Café Madeleine	35 Pl. Madeleine	Madeleine	p. 69
Madeleine	Espace Café Bleu	15 rue du Fbg-St.-Honoré	Madeleine	p. 68
Madeleine	Fauchon	26 Pl. Madeleine	Madeleine	p. 69
Madeleine	Ladurée	16 rue Royale	Madeleine	p. 70
Madeleine	Paris-London, Le	16 Pl. Madeleine	Madeleine	p. 69
Madeleine	Peny, Le	3 Pl. Madeleine	Madeleine	p. 105
Montparnasse	Closerie des Lilas	171 bd. Montparnasse	Port-Royal	p. 12
Montparnasse	Coupole, La	102 bd. Montparnasse	Vavin	p. 12
Montparnasse	Dôme, Le	106 bd. Montparnasse	Vavin	p. 12
Montparnasse	Doucet	25 rue d'Assas	St.-Placide	p. 140
Montparnasse	Rotonde, La	105 bd. Montparnasse	Vavin	p. 14
Montparnasse	Sélect, Le	99 bd. Montparnasse	Vavin	p. 95
Moulin Rouge	Batifol	3 Pl. Blanche	Blanche	p. 128
Moulin Rouge	Sans-Souci, Le	65 rue Pigalle	Pigalle	p. 85
Musée d'Orsay	Bar du Pont Royal	7 rue Montalembert	Rue du Bac	p. 38
Notre Dame	Café Notre-Dame	21 Quai Monte bello	Cité	p. 124
Notre Dame	Quasimodo N.-D.	11 rue d'Arcole	Cité	p. 124
Notre Dame	Bar du Caveau	17 Place Dauphine	Cité	p. 49
Opéra (Garnier)	Entr'acte, L'	1 rue Auber	Opéra	p. 68
Opéra (Garnier)	Grain de Café, Le	4 Pl. de l'Opéra	Opéra	p. 71
Opéra (Garnier)	Malongo; Café, in Lafayette Gourmet (Monoprix)	93 rue de Provence	Opéra	p. 119

Attraction	Café	Address	Métro	Page
Opéra (Garnier)	Paix, Café de la	12 bd. Capucines	Opéra	p. 68
Opéra (Garnier)	Relais des Galeries (Gal. Lafayette)	40 bd. Haussmann	Opéra	p. 106
Orly Airport	Bagatelle Café	Orly Sud Airport	RER Orlyrail	p. 131
Père Lachaise	Saint Amour, Le	32 bd. Ménilmontant	Père Lachaise	p. 135
Pigalle	Batifol	3 Place Blanche	Blanche	p. 128
Place des Vosges	Petit Fer à Cheval	30 rue Vieille du Temple	St.-Paul	p. 95
Place des Vosges	Café des Musées	49 rue de Turenne	Chemin Vert	p. 46
Place des Vosges	Enfants Gâtés, Les	43 rue Francs-Bourgeois	St.-Paul	p. 47
Place des Vosges	Locandiera Bar	27 rue de Turenne	St.-Paul	p. 123
Place des Vosges	Ma Bourgogne	19 Place des Vosges	St.-Paul	*
Place des Vosges	Martini, Café	11 rue Pas de Mule	Chemin Vert	p. 48
Place des Vosges	Olivier, L' (resto)	6 rue Birague	St.-Paul/Bastille	p. 142
Place des Vosges	Vieux Comptoir	8 rue Birague	St.-Paul	p. 142
Place Vendôme	Bar Louis le Grand	1 rue Louis le Grand	Opéra	p. 59
Place Vendôme	Castiglione, Le	235 rue St.-Honoré	Concorde	p. 58
Place Vendôme	Colombe, La	2 rue de la Paix	Opéra	p. 58
Place Vendôme	Ver Luisant, Au	26 rue Mont Thabor	Palais-Royal	p. 59
République	Café Le Paris	24 bd. Richard-Lenoir	Bréguet-Sabin	p. 22
République	Royal République, Le	11 Pl. de la République	République	p. 129

* Not mentioned in the text, but convenient to the attraction

Cafés by Nearest Attraction

Attraction	Café	Address	Métro	Page
République	Relais d'Eguisheim, Le	6 Pl. de la République	République	p. 42
République	Taverne, Bar Belge	5 Pl. de la République	République	p. 129
République	Thermomètre, Le	4 Pl. de la République	République	p. 42
Sacré Coeur	Balto, Le	58 rue Custine	Jules Joffrin	p. 129
Sacré Coeur	Bohème du Tertre	2 Pl. du Tertre	Anvers/Funicular	p. 76
Sacré Coeur	Carrousel, Le	8 rue des 3 Frères	Abbesses	p. 75
Sacré Coeur	Clairon des Chasseurs	3 Pl. du Tertre	Anvers/Funicular	p. 76
Sacré Coeur	Crêpe à Pic, La	35 rue Lepic	Blanche	p. 130
Sacré Coeur	Gavroche, Le	22 rue Hermel	Jules Joffrin	p. 130
Sacré Coeur	Lapin Agile, Le	22 rue des Saules	Lamrck-Caulaincrt	p. 92
Sacré Coeur	Mère Catherine, La	6 Pl. du Tertre	Anvers/Funicular	p. 75
Sacré Coeur	Négociants, Aux	27 rue Lambert	Château-Rouge	p. 75
Sacré Coeur	Nord-Sud, Le	79 rue Mont Cenis	Jules Joffrin	p. 75
Sacré Coeur	Petit Café de Montmartre	10 rue Fontaine du Butte	Lamarck-Caulainct	*
Sacré Coeur	Relais, Au	48 rue Lamark	Lamark-Caulainct	p. 75
Sacré Coeur	Tabac de la Mairie	28 rue Hermel	Jules Joffrin	p. 92
Sacré Coeur	Tire Bouchon, Au	7 rue Norvins	Anvers/Funicular	*
Saint-Eustache	Café du Croissant	146 rue Montmartre	Sentier	p. 141
Saint-Eustache	Cochon à l'Oreille, Le	15 rue Montmartre	Châtelet	p. 96
Saint-Eustache	Tambour, Le	41 rue Montmartre	Châtelet/Sentier	p. 38
Saint-Germain	Danton, Le	103 bd. St.-Germain	Odéon	p. 15
Saint-Germain	Brasserie Lipp	151 bd. St.-Germain	St.-Germain	p. 13
Saint-Germain	Mabillon, Le	164 bd. St.-Germain	St.-Germain	*

* Not mentioned in the text, but convenient to the attraction

157

Attraction	Café	Address	Métro	Page
Saint-Germain	Boul' Mich, Le	116 bd. St.-Germain	St.-Germain	p. 15
Saint-Germain	Calumet, Le	30 Notre-Dame-des-Champs	N-D-des-Champs	p. 14
Saint-Germain	Pré aux Clercs, Le	30 rue Bonaparte	St.-Germain	p. 15
Saint-Germain	Brasserie L'Atlas	11 rue de Buci	Mabillon	p. 57
Saint-Germain	Flore, Le	172 bd. St-Germain	St.-Germain	p. 35
Saint-Germain	Palette, La	43 rue de Seine	Odéon	p. 97
Saint-Germain	Deux Magots, Les	6 Pl. St.-Germain	St.-Germain	p. 13
Saint-Germain	Rhumerie, La	166 bd. St.-Germain	St.-Germain	p. 57
Saint-Germain	Saint-André, Le	2 rue Danton	St.-Michel	p. 15
Saint-Sulpice	Vieux Colombier, Au	65 rue de Rennes	Rennes/St.-Placide	p. 14
Saint-Sulpice	Lina's Sandwiches	27 rue St.-Sulpice	St.-Sulpice	p. 119
Saint-Sulpice	Mairie, Café de la	8 Pl. St.-Sulpice	St.-Sulpice	p. 37
Saint-Sulpice	Côté Jardin	22 rue de Sèvres	Sèvres-Babylone	p. 107
Saint-Sulpice	Latin Odéon	126 bd. St.-Germain	Odéon	p. 58
Saint-Sulpice	Mazet, Le	61 rue St.-André-des-Arts	Odéon	p. 58
Saint-Sulpice	Procope, Le	13 rue de l'Anc. Comédie	Odéon	p. 24
Saint-Sulpice	Relais Odéon	132 bd. St.-Germain	Odéon	p. 24
Sainte-Chapelle	Deux Palais, Les	3 bd. du Palais	Cité	p. 49
Sainte-Chapelle	Ecluse, L'	15 quai Grands-Augustins	St.-Michel	p. 57
Sainte-Chapelle	Bar du Caveau	17 Pl. Dauphine	Pont-Neuf	p. 49
Sainte-Trinité	Boeuf à la Mode	32 rue La Bruyère	St.-Georges/Trinité	*

158

* Not mentioned in the text, but convenient to the attraction

Bibliography

Allan, Tony. *Americans in Paris*. Chicago: Contemporary Books Inc., 1977.
Allais, Alphonse. *En verve*. Edited by François Caraduc. Paris: Pierre Horay, 1970.
Allais, Alphonse. "Utilité à Paris du bottin des départements." *Trésors du rire*. Edited by François Caraduc. Paris: Pierre Horay, 1970.

Baedeker, Karl. *Paris and Environs*. Leipzig: Karl Baedeker, 1904.
Baker, Tim. "Paris Cafés." *The Paris Free Voice*. July-August 1994.
Bair, Deirdre. *Simone de Beauvoir*. New York: Summit Books, 1990.
Barry, Joseph A. *Paris and Parisians*. New York: W. W. Norton, 1951.
Barry, Joseph A. *The People of Paris*. New York: Doubleday, 1966.
Beauvoir, Simone de. *The Prime of Life*. Translated by Peter Green. Cleveland: World Publishing Company, 1962. Originally published by Librairie Gallimard, 1960.
Béchaz, André. "Paris sur zinc." *L'Express Paris*. June 1–7, 1990.
Bernier, Georges. *Paris Cafés*. New York: Wildenstein, 1985.
Bernier, Olivier. *Fireworks at Dusk: Paris in the Thirties*. Boston: Little, Brown and Company, 1993.
Bresler, Fenton. *The Mystery of Georges Simenon*. New York: Beaufort Books Inc., 1983.

Carco, Francis. *La belle époque au temps de Bruant*. Paris: Gallimard, 1954.
Callaghan, Morley. *That Summer in Paris*. New York: Dell Publishing Company, 1963.
Cody, Morrill. *This Must Be the Place: Memoirs of Montparnasse Related by Jimmy Charters*. London: Herbert Joseph, Ltd., 1934.
Conway, John Joseph. *Americans in Paris*. New York: John Lane, 1912.
Courtine, Robert. *Le ventre de Paris*. Paris: Librairie Academique Perrin, 1985.

Bibliography

Courthion, Pierre. *Montmartre.* Translated by Stuart Gilbert. Paris: Skira, 1956.

Crespelle, Jean-Paul. *La vie quotidienne à Montparnasse, 1905–1930.* Paris: Hachette, 1976.

Dictionnaire de Paris. Paris: Librairie Larousse. 1964.

Eibel, Alfred. "L'itinéraire des poètes." *Le Quotidien de Paris.* July 25, 1990.

Fitch, Noel Riley. *Walks in Hemingway's Paris.* New York: St. Martin's Press, 1989.

Ford, Hugh. *Four Lives in Paris.* San Francisco: Point Press, 1987.

Garrioch, David. *Neighbourhood and Community in Paris, 1740–1790.* Cambridge: Cambridge University Press, 1986.

Gault, Henry and Millau, Christian. *The Best of Paris.* Los Angeles: Gault Millau Inc., 1993.

Grierson, Francis. *Parisian Portraits.* London: John Lane, the Bodley Head, 1913.

Hayman, Ronald. *Sartre: A Life.* New York: Simon and Schuster, 1987.

Henry, Stuart. *Paris Days and Evenings.* Philadelphia: J. B. Lippincott, 1896.

The Home Book of Quotations. Selected by Burton Stevenson. New York: Dodd, Mead & Company, 1967.

Himes, Chester. *My Life of Absurdity,* Vol. 2. Garden City: Doubleday & Company, 1976.

Huddleston, Sisley. *Paris Salons, Cafés, Studios.* Philadelphia: J. B. Lippincott, 1928.

James, Henry. *Parisian Sketches.* New York: New York University Press, 1957.

Jarnac, Isabelle Dillmann de. "Rencontrer Paris-Passions: Françoise Cachin." *Paris le Journal,* Journal d'information de la ville de Paris, no. 44 (July 15, 1994).

"La Route des Zincs." *Figaroscope.* November 11–17, 1992.

The Left Bank Revisited: Selections from the Paris Tribune, 1917–1943. Edited by Hugh Ford. University Park and London: Pennsylvania State University Press, 1972.

Liebling, A. J. *Between Meals.* Guernsey: The Guernsey Press, 1986.

Littlewood, Ian. *Paris: A Literary Companion.* London: John Murray, 1987.

Morley, Robert. *A Musing Morley.* London: Robson Books, 1974.

Bibliography

Nord, Philip G. *Paris Shopkeepers and the Politics of Resentment.* Princeton: Princeton University Press, 1986.

Oberthur, Mariel. *Cafés and Cabarets of Montmartre.* Salt Lake City: Peregrine Smith Books, 1984.

Perruchot, Henri. *Toulouse-Lautrec.* Cleveland: World Publishing Company, 1960. Originally published by Hachette, 1958.
Putnam, Samuel. *Paris Was Our Mistress.* New York: Viking Press, 1947.

Reid, Alexander. *Paris.* South Brunswick: A.S. Barnes and Co., 1965.
Rice, Howard C., Jr. *Thomas Jefferson's Paris.* Princeton: Princeton University Press, 1976.
Rudorff, Raymond. *Belle Epoque: Paris in the Nineties.* London: Hamish Hamilton, 1972.

Shelley, Henry. *Old Paris.* Boston: L. C. Page, 1912.
Simenon, Georges. *Maigret's Dead Man.* Translated by Jean Stewart. New York: Doubleday & Company, 1964.
Simenon, Georges. *Maigret and the Lazy Burglar.* Translated by Daphne Woodward and Robert Eglesfield. New York: Harcourt Brace, 1994.
Skinner, Cornelia Otis. *Elegant Wits and Grand Horizontals.* Boston: Houghton Mifflin Company, 1962.
Street, Julien. *Where Paris Dines.* Garden City: Doubleday, Doran and Company, 1929.

Walter, Gérard. *Paris Under the Occupation.* Translated by Tony White. New York: Orion Press, 1960.
Wells, Patricia. *Food Lover's Guide to Paris.* New York: Workman Publishing, 1984.
Wickes, George. *Americans in Paris.* Garden City: Doubleday and Company, 1969.
Wiser, William. *The Crazy Years.* New York: Atheneum, 1983.
Writers at Work: The Paris Review Interviews. Edited by George Plimpton. Harmondsworth: Penguin Books, 1963.
Wylie, Laurence. *Village in the Vaucluse.* Cambridge, Mass.: Harvard University Press, 1957.

Index

* Outstanding cafés/ bistros, worth a special trip

Index